Routledge Library Editions

OVERHEAD COSTS

T0358415

ECONOMICS

Routledge Library Editions – Economics

DEVELOPMENT ECONOMICS
In 7 Volumes

OVERHEAD COSTS

Some Essays in Economic Analysis

W ARTHUR LEWIS

Routledge
Taylor & Francis Group

LONDON AND NEW YORK

First published in 1949

Reprinted in 2003 by
Routledge
2 Park Square, Milton Park, Abingdon, Oxon, OX14 4RN
or
270 Madison Avenue, New York, NY 10016

First issued in paperback 2010

Routledge is an imprint of the Taylor & Francis Group

The publishers have made every effort to contact authors/copyright holders
of the works reprinted in *Routledge Library Editions – Economics*. This has
not been possible in every case, however, and we would welcome
correspondence from those individuals/companies we have been unable to
trace.

These reprints are taken from original copies of each book. In many cases
the condition of these originals is not perfect. The publisher has gone to
great lengths to ensure the quality of these reprints, but wishes to point
out that certain characteristics of the original copies will, of necessity, be
apparent in reprints thereof.

British Library Cataloguing in Publication Data
A CIP catalogue record for this book
is available from the British Library

Overhead Costs
ISBN 978-0-415-31300-1 (hbk)
ISBN 978-0-415-60697-4 (pbk)
ISBN 978-0-415-31294-3 (set)

Miniset: Development Economics

Series: Routledge Library Editions – Economics

OVERHEAD COSTS

SOME ESSAYS IN
ECONOMIC ANALYSIS

by

W. ARTHUR LEWIS

Professor of Economics
in the University of Manchester

Routledge
Taylor & Francis Group

LONDON AND NEW YORK

PREFACE

Each of the seven chapters of this book deals with a problem that arises out of the existence of overhead costs, but the book is neither a systematic nor an exhaustive treatise on that enormous subject.

The first paper, on "Fixed Costs," is principally concerned with competition between road and rail transport, which is a difficult problem; but I have put it first because it begins with a general survey of problems arising out of overhead costs. Readers new to the subject will find it easier to tackle some of the other chapters first.

The essays have seemed to need less revision than I had expected, bearing in mind that they were written over a period of seven years. The biggest change is in "The Two-Part Tariff," where I have elaborated the analysis of the peak, without altering the substance of the argument. The last essay, "The Administration of Socialist Enterprises," was not written until I came to prepare the other material for publication as a book.

It was Professor Sir Arnold Plant who first interested me in these problems, and to him I owe inspiration, first insights, and much happy disputation. On many problems our emphases, and therefore our practical conclusions, are different, and he must not be identified with any opinions expressed here.

Thanks are due to the Editors of *Economica* and of *The Modern Law Review* for permission to reprint.

February 1948.   W. A. L.

CONTENTS

CHAPTER I

FIXED COSTS

This chapter is concerned with the case where similar services are supplied by two different industries, one or both of which has a high ratio of fixed to variable expenses. Gas and electricity and road and rail transport are the outstanding examples, and special reference will be made to them. It has always seemed difficult to fit this type of case into the general rule that price should equal marginal cost because it has never been clear what marginal cost means in such contexts. The first problem is therefore to define the line between marginal and fixed costs.

I

THE ANATOMY OF FIXED COSTS

1. In welfare economics the cost of something is the value to other producers of the resources which are used to produce it; cost is measured by computing what expenses would be saved if production were curtailed and resources released for use elsewhere. This cost differs from cost in the business or accounting sense, which is simply the sum expended on production, because there are expenses which the business man cannot escape by curtailing his output—e.g. the sum invested in specific equipment which is no longer required. The economist's costs are those which can be escaped; fixed costs are those which cannot: escapability is the essence of the distinction. It is not, however, a simple distinction, because some costs are escapable in some senses but not in others, and we must spend a little time on it.

Fixed or inescapable costs fall into four categories:

(a) some are inescapable in the short run but not in the long run;

(b) some are joint costs, and inescapable only in that sense;

(c) some are inescapable for small but not for large changes of output; and

(d) some are inescapable in all senses.

2. An entrepreneur makes commitments in relation to the level of output which he expects, and once he has committed himself

to expenses appropriate to that level, he finds that some of his commitments cannot be altered rapidly even if output contracts permanently to a lower level. Some commitments can be escaped at once, but others take time. His commitments are of two classes; commitments under contracts to hire, and commitments by purchase, by investment in construction, or by other methods of capital creation.

Commitments under hiring contracts are the easier class. All such contracts, whether for manual labour, for administrative staff, for machinery, buildings, or for other services, have a time limit. The contract may be escapable at once, because the time limit is short, or because there is provision for discharging it at short notice or because obligations under it (e.g. a lease) can be transferred. The cost immediately escapable may not be as great as that which can be escaped ultimately, when the contract expires, if there is some penalty for immediate discharge, or some loss on transferring the obligations; and the contract may be continued temporarily. But sooner or later the contract expires, and with that comes complete escape.

Investments in assets are more complicated. With these, too, immediate escape is often possible, and its neglect has been one of the commoner errors in economic discussion. The immediately escapable cost is user cost.[1] This may not be as great as that

---

[1] This is a difficult concept. User cost for any year (or unit of output) can be computed as follows.

(i) The asset can be sold, and the present value of its expected yields in each future year of life, plus its scrap value (also discounted), must exceed the price for which it can be sold. Assume n years of working life; if life is determined by obsolescence, the relevant yields are those of the first n years, but if it is determined by wear and tear, the relevant yields are those of the n most profitable years (after discounting). The corollary is that the yield expected this year must equal at least the difference between the price and the expected yield of the remaining $(n - 1)$ years of working life plus scrap value, if this difference is positive. This is the minimum value of this year's user cost. If the price is not greater than the sum expected in the other $(n - 1)$ years, this minimum user cost is zero.

(ii) This year's yield must also exceed the difference between the price that could be obtained for the asset this year and next year's price if used this year. If this year's expected yield exceeds the sum stipulated in (i) but not this sum, the time pattern of yields in outside uses is different from the time pattern of yields here, and the asset should be used elsewhere this year and returned to use here next year (but this assumes physical wear and tear this year to be the same in either use).

(iii) This year's yield must also exceed the expected yield from any future

which can be escaped when the asset expires and its replacement falls due. Thus hiring contracts and assets are in the same category. Nearly all commitments are immediately escapable, but the cost escapable now may not be as great as that which can be escaped ultimately when the commitment has expired and a new commitment is necessary if production is to continue. Assets differ from hiring contracts only in that a small percentage of assets are of infinite durability, and with these there is only an immediately escapable cost to consider.[1]

The distinction between short-run and long-run cost corresponds to this distinction between immediately and ultimately escapable cost. In practice, however, neither of these distinctions is as simple as is currently implied. Some commitments expire at once, some next week, some next month, some next year, and so on. Escapable cost is not just short-run and long-run, immediate and ultimate. It varies for as far ahead as you care to look. Furthermore, it does not vary continuously with time. If commitments of equal cost significance expired in constant procession, one in each month, and if renewal could then be put on to a month-to-month basis, short-term cost would rise month by month steadily nearer to long-term cost, until all commitments were on a monthly basis. But none of these conditions is fulfilled. The dates at which commitments expire have no regular pattern, and the sums involved vary widely, so that the fluctuations in short-run cost are arbitrary accidents. Then, as each commitment falls due for renewal, say for x years, all those due to expire during those x years have to be considered, since if any of those will not pay and

year which is excluded from use by this year's use. If working life is determined by obsolescence, the value of this is zero. If it is determined by wear and tear, this year must be one of the n most profitable; user cost is the yield of the $(n + 1)$th most profitable year. (This assumes that in its effect on the life of the machine use in any one year is a perfect substitute for use in any other. The problem is more complicated but not insoluble if this is not so.)

This gives us three minimum values for user cost. The relevant one is whichever is the largest. User cost can be zero if obsolescence determines life, if the value in outside uses is small relatively to value here, and if the value in outside uses does not diminish. It cannot be zero if life is determined by wear and tear, for it must then equal at least the yield of the $(n + 1)$th year.

[1] The easier escape from hiring contracts may also be illusory. From the point of view of social cost it is irrelevant whether an asset is hired or purchased; what matters is whether it is specific or not. E.g. if specific labour is dismissed the entrepreneur escapes a private cost, its wage, but if the labour simply becomes unemployed, there is no social saving.

will be discontinued, this may not pay either. The expiry of a single commitment may therefore bring large numbers under review and cause a great jump in immediately escapable cost. And, as each commitment is renewed, short-run cost, which had risen high to include renewal cost, now sinks again to the level of the temporarily inescapable. There is no such quantity as "the marginal cost" of output; there is not even a simple choice between two quantities, short- and long-run cost; there is a large variety of costs to choose from, depending merely on how far ahead you choose to look, and this collection of costs itself varies from day to day, as current commitments alter.

3. Some costs are inescapable only in the sense that they are joint costs. For example, the traffic from A to B may be permanently in excess of the traffic from B to A, and some vehicles will always be returning empty. The marginal cost of using those vehicles is small, and the inescapable cost is heavy. If, however, there were no traffic from A to B, the cost of running from B to A would be easily escapable, and it is inescapable only because it is a joint cost with the cost of running to B. Where there are joint costs neither can be considered escapable or inescapable by itself. Together, the joint cost is escapable; separately, the cost of each part has to be found by difference, by subtracting the yield of the others from the total cost.

Depreciation is one of the most important cases of a joint cost inescapable only in this sense. When an entrepreneur is considering adding extra equipment to his undertaking, he knows that it may yield output in each year of its life, but he is unable to allocate a cost to the output of any one year except by considering the yields of other years. Each year's use, assuming the investment made, has a user cost, but the sum of these user costs may be much less than the cost of the asset, and the difference cannot be allocated to each year, but must be recouped from surpluses. If the industry were expected to be in stationary equilibrium, the amortisation attributable to each year would be easily calculable. Since there is stationary equilibrium, the amount of the surplus in each year is the same, and it must be a sum which, deducting interest on the cost of the equipment, will, when invested yearly at compound interest, yield at the end of the life of the equipment a sum equal to its cost less scrap value. But where conditions are expected to fluctuate, so will the surplus. It may be that the equipment can be kept fully occupied throughout its life, but only by charging different prices at different times, high when demand is strong, and low while it is weak, so that the surplus will sometimes be great and sometimes be small; but again it must be expected that the sum of these surpluses, at the appropriate rate of interest, will equal the cost. It may even be that in some periods no price that would yield any surplus is low enough to keep demand at the level that will occupy the equipment; then the installation of the equipment is justified only if it is expected that the surpluses when demand is strong will be adequate when summed to cover the entire cost. This is only another way of saying that where fluctuations in output are expected, the cost of the equipment, looking ahead before investment is made, is attributable only to periods when it is fully occupied—the entire cost is chargeable to the peaks in proportions depending on what charge keeps the peaks fully occupied.[1]

The net result is that, before any commitment is made, it may be foreseen that there will be successive periods of full and excess capacity. In periods of excess capacity marginal output will give rise to smaller escapable costs than in periods of full capacity,[1] but cost at such periods will be inescapable only in the sense of being a joint cost with other periods.

4. The third category of inescapable commitments consists of those where an expense does not vary with output because it is indivisible. Indivisibility need not be identified with some concrete piece of equipment; it may merely be that a certain expense varies with output, but in smaller proportion. The indivisible element is the difference between the total expense and the product of quantity-of-output times marginal cost, and will itself vary with output if marginal cost is not constant.

Indivisible expenses and fixed costs are frequently taken as synonymous, but they are not. Fixed costs are those which are inescapable, and indivisible costs may be immediately escapable. A railway can decide to run more or fewer carriages, or trains, or to keep open more or fewer stations, or, taking the matter to its

---

[1] This assumes that life is determined by obsolescence, and that off-peak user cost is zero. If life is determined by obsolescence, off-peak user cost may be zero. If it is determined by wear and tear, off-peak use is at the expense of later peak use, and off-peak use now therefore has the same user cost as peak use now, and there is no difference between peak and off-peak escapable cost. The problems that arise from regular fluctuations in demand are more fully discussed in Chapter II

logical conclusion, to close down altogether. Whatever the indivisible unit, if the expenses attributable to it are escapable, they must be covered if the unit is to be maintained. Confusion on this point has been due to a tacit acceptance of the unit of product as being the unit on which the calculation of economic cost must be based. But there is no greater significance attaching to the passenger in transport than there is to one or other of the indivisible units required for his conveyance, and if the cost of any unit is escapable it must be covered, even though the marginal cost of the product is zero. Marginal cost is not the only real social cost, and indivisible cost is not necessarily fixed.[1]

5. When we say that some costs are inescapable in all senses, we naturally refer to commitments which have already been made, since all costs are escapable *ex-ante*. If in any given situation where commitments have been made we include in escapable costs, long-run escapable and not merely short-run costs, escapable joint costs, and escapable indivisible costs, we are left with two classes of inescapable costs, which constitute the difference between cost to the economist and cost in the accounting sense.

[1] A good deal of the current analysis of monopoly makes nonsense of itself because it fails to recognise this. All costs but marginal costs are said to be relevant only in the long run, whereas indivisible costs are relevant to even the most short-run analysis to the same extent as divisible ones, i.e. to the extent to which they are immediately escapable. Entrepreneurs regard most of their overhead costs as escapable indivisible expenses, and refuse to produce unless they are covered. Economists who think that only marginal costs should count regard this obstinacy with a mixture of surprise, pain and contempt, and are driven to explain it away by calculating "the degree of monopoly power." No fruitful analysis of monopoly can be based on marginal cost only.

In this respect public utility engineers are well ahead of most economists who write on the theory of costs. The latter usually treat costs as being a function of output only. The former divide costs into those which vary with output, demand related standing costs, customer costs, and the residue. The first is generally known as prime cost. The concept of demand related costs is another way of expressing the fact that cost cannot be computed unless we know whether the supply will be taken at the peak or not, and actually the economist's marginal cost can be adapted to take care of this (though it usually is not). Customer costs are indivisible costs varying with the number of customers and not with the amount each takes, e.g. the cost of wiring houses. The residue is the difference between the total and the other three. The simple view of cost as a function of quantity of output only, which elevates marginal cost to the rank of being the only social cost that matters, originates from theories in which all factors of production are assumed to be divisible and non-specific; its transfer to fields where there is a high ratio of fixed costs is untenable.

First, we have included in long-run escapable costs all assets which have to be renewed. That leaves us with assets which do not have to be renewed. There are two classes of these, permanent assets and assets which are not renewed only because demand does not justify renewal. Taking permanent assets first, the analysis depends on whether the amount of these varies with output, i.e. they are divisible (e.g. the amount of land required for rail or road tracks depends on the amount of traffic) or whether they are indivisible (e.g. the legal expenses of floating a company). (a) The use of permanent indivisible assets gives rise to no social cost, unless these assets are useful in some other industry; the difference between the price that they would fetch and their original cost is a cost in the accounting but not in the economic sense. (b) Whether the use of divisible permanent assets gives rise to social cost, over and above sale value in other uses, depends on whether the undertaking is working to capacity or not. For example, if it is, and an increase in traffic requires the purchase of further land, the cost of land varies with traffic and enters into marginal cost, but if the undertaking is working below capacity, and existing tracks can take further traffic, the cost of land does not enter into marginal cost, and is an accounting but not a social cost (apart from its value in other uses). (c) Then there are assets which are not permanent by nature, but which are not being renewed because demand has contracted. E.g. if demand has contracted 25 per cent, the renewable 75 per cent enters into long-run escapable cost, but the other 25 per cent does not, and is an accounting but not a social cost.

The other main source of difference is that accountants are concerned with original cost, but economists with replacement cost. When the latter is below the former, escapable cost is less than original cost. The financial difficulties of this will be referred to in the next section.

II

COST AND PRICE

1. It has now become an axiom that if the price mechanism is accurately to allocate resources, price must equal marginal cost, and recent writers have said even that this rule simplifies the administration of State undertakings since it is virtually the only instruction that need be given to managers to determine output.

We are now in a position to grapple with some of its hidden difficulties.

They are four, corresponding to the categories of fixed cost:

(a) the fact that there is a whole range of marginal costs, depending on how far ahead one looks;

(b) the fact that marginal cost may fluctuate from one moment to the next;

(c) the fact that indivisible escapable costs must be covered; and

(d) the fact that the accounting and the economic cost are different.

2. If an industry is working at full capacity the immediately and the ultimately escapable marginal costs coincide. But if there is excess capacity, the immediately escapable may be less than what is ultimately escapable as contracts or assets expire, and looking ahead, there is a whole range of marginal costs from which to choose.

In perfect competition price equals the immediately escapable marginal cost and fluctuates with it. There is one exception. It may be that at a price adequate to cover renewals demand would not be sufficient to occupy all the equipment, but that at a price equal only to immediately escapable cost it would occupy more equipment than is in existence. This is the familiar case where short-run marginal cost rises vertically as full capacity is reached. In this case price will exceed short-run marginal cost, but be less than long-run marginal cost, to an extent depending on elasticity of demand.

The case for basing price in conditions of excess capacity on the immediately escapable cost is that the fullest use is thereby made of existing resources. Suppose, for example, that demand contracts in an industry where the equipment is specific but ultimately renewable. Sooner or later the workable equipment will contract and an equilibrium price be established adequate to cover renewals. But if the price is maintained at that level in the immediate present, while there is excess capacity, some demands which would willingly have paid immediate marginal cost may be excluded at a price equal to long-run marginal cost, and specific equipment is less utilised than it ought to be—a loss of output which continues as long as the equipment lasts, but no longer.

Against this advantage must be set a disadvantage. If the price is fixed at immediate marginal cost so long as the excess capacity lasts, the industry makes a loss not only on the excess capacity, but on all the specific equipment used, including that proportion which is permanently needed, and which must be renewed. There may only, from the long-run point of view, be 10 per cent excess capacity, but the industry will be unable to earn full amortisation quotas even on the 90 per cent which has to be renewed. This transfer of income to the consumer is a gift which he never expected, to which he has no particular right, and which he will receive only temporarily while the excess capacity lasts. The consequences of this are more serious than a mere transfer of income from investor to consumer, for an industry which does not earn its amortisation quotas may have difficulty in renewing the 90 per cent capacity that ought to be renewed, partly because in these days internal reserves are so large a part of the total new investment, partly because, since it has been making losses for some time people will be reluctant to invest in it even though there is a case for a 90 per cent reinvestment, and partly because it is particularly difficult to obtain monies for new investment when an equal or prior claim on all returns must go to existing share and debenture holders who require satisfaction in respect of investments that still have not paid—a difficulty escapable only if a firm is reconstructed every time such circumstances occur.

If price were based not on short-run but on long-run marginal cost, no demands would be served that could not in the long run be maintained, but full amortisation would be earned on all assets which must be renewed, and only to the extent that renewal is needed. Where there are no close substitutes for the product this would probably make little difference to the output of the industry,[1] since demands are not as elastic in the short run as we like to think. Where two similar industries are competing, e.g. road and rail, it will make little difference to their joint output, but the distribution of that output between them may be significantly affected. For example, suppose a long-run trend in favour of road transport at the expense of rail transport. Then if rail charges are based always on long-run cost, road transport will be larger than it would be if rail charges were based on short-run cost, and it will always be larger than it ought strictly to be. But the difference is

---

[1] Apart from income effects; consumers will not have made a windfall gain from investors, and to the extent to which their expenditure patterns are different, outputs of the industries on which they would spend are affected. There will also be short-run differences in the propensity to consume.

B

only one of time; at any moment the situation will be in long-run (moving) equilibrium instead of still on the move towards it—adjustment is speeded up, but is faster than it should be. It is not obvious that this disadvantage is greater than the disadvantage of having an industry unable to earn amortisation quotas which it will require.

More serious might be the repercussions on the process of eliminating excess capacity. If price equals only immediately escapable cost, the loss of amortisation quotas is a powerful eliminator of redundant firms, though experience shows that the agony may be very long-drawn-out, and that it is not always the right firms that disappear. If price is to be kept at the level of long-run cost the marginal firms are not so easily dislodged, and some scheme for the elimination of the less efficient may have to be applied unless the differences in efficiency are marked. The technical difficulties and the cost of applying such a scheme have to be considered, and may well be decisive in industries where competition on the basis of short-run costs would be fairly rapidly effective. But where we are considering public utilities or State enterprises operated as monopolies, this kind of consideration is hardly relevant, since it is not whole firms that have to be eliminated but parts of a single firm. In such cases the earning of needed amortisation quotas seems the decisive issue.

3. The second difficulty is that where there are fluctuations in demand or supply there will be fluctuations in price. This will be so if price is equal to immediately escapable cost, because that necessarily alters with the passage of time. But it will also be so even in cases where there is no permanent excess capacity, but only periods of temporary excess capacity which are foreseen before the commitment is made, and which are therefore part of the long-run equilibrium situation.

Regular price fluctuations are not much of a problem. It is not always technically possible to arrange for such fluctuations; e.g. in electricity this requires a meter which records the amount consumed in each part of each day of the year, and such meters were not invented until fairly late in the history of the industry. Neither is it always convenient that the price fluctuations should follow changes in demand too closely. Consider, for example, the situation in suburban passenger transport. At the peak hour of the morning the 'bus travels into the city packed; since it has to return to its depot, the marginal cost of taking persons out of the city is negligible, and if price is to be based on marginal cost they should travel practically for nothing. As the peak passes, however, the balance of inward and outward passengers begins to be readjusted; gradually the fare to the city should fall, and the fare from the city rise; and in the evening the fare out should cover nearly all costs, and the fare in be virtually zero. Fares which followed the changes in the balance of traffics too closely would be a nuisance, and most people would prefer a limited number of changes (if any) which only broadly reflected the changing costs. Allowing for these difficulties, regular and foreseeable fluctuations in price are not much of a problem.

Irregular and unforeseeable fluctuations are, however, a nuisance. Such fluctuations are not so great a nuisance in respect of commodities or services where an organised market can be built up, such as cotton or tramp shipping, especially if the organisation can include a futures market, but they are certainly a nuisance in other fields. This is so partly because in an uncertain world one likes to have as many certainties as possible. But it is also partly because, where prices fluctuate the consumer tends to suspect discrimination, and to feel that the price may have risen at the moment he arrives not solely because the impersonal supply and demand factors have changed, but rather because he personally is not as favoured a buyer as someone else. This is one of the reasons why uniform prices have been enforced by the law on railways and taxicabs, and by custom on department stores, hotels, professional men, and in many other fields.

Here again we have to compare the advantage of securing fullest hour-by-hour utilisation of resources with other disadvantages. Foreseeable regular changes in price are fully allowable, but the case for evening out the irregular fluctuations seems to be overwhelming, at least in public utility industries.

4. The third difficulty in equating price to marginal cost is that it leaves uncovered escapable indivisible expenses which ought to be covered if the retention of these resources by the consumers of this commodity is to be justified. Where there are escapable indivisible expenses the rule that price must equal marginal cost is inadequate; the rule should be rather that price must be not less than marginal cost, and there must be enough surplus to cover escapable indivisible expenses. This is obvious enough if the indivisible cost is a "customer cost," incurred for one customer only, e.g. the cost of connecting his house for electricity, which does not

vary with the amount consumed. But it applies equally if the indivisible cost benefits a number of consumers, e.g. the laying of a main for the whole street, or all the consumers. The method of charging which most nearly secures the correct allocation of resources is the two-part tariff, with the variable charge equal to divisible marginal cost, and the fixed charge taking from each consumer the customer cost plus, as contribution to the indivisible expenses, such amount as he can afford to pay. The second nearest approach is price discrimination. Charging the same price to all buyers comes, from this point of view, a poor third.

These methods of charging recover the indivisible cost from consumers' surplus. There may also be a producers' surplus from which it might be recovered. A producers' surplus will exist if marginal cost is rising, and it is important to distinguish different types of surplus. Marginal cost may be rising because applying more of the variable to the indivisible factors yields diminishing returns; or it may be rising because the price of the variable factors rises as more is purchased. In the former case the producers' surplus accrues to the undertaking. As we defined an indivisible cost not as the cost of an indivisible factor, but as the difference between the total expense and the product of quantity-of-output times marginal cost, we have already deducted this surplus in order to arrive at the indivisible cost, and therefore no contribution is available from this type of producers' surplus. If marginal cost rises so fast as to equal or exceed average cost, there will be no indivisible cost in this sense, though there may be indivisible factors. If marginal cost is rising because some variable factor is in inelastic supply, the surplus will be accruing to the undertaking if the variable factor is an asset of which it is purchasing or hiring successive units at rising prices; but it will be accruing to the owners of the factors in the hiring or purchase of which no discrimination is possible. All surpluses accruing to the undertaking are already accounted for. The only producers' surpluses available for consideration are therefore those which accrue to outside owners.[1] Another producers' surplus of this kind may exist even if the factor is not in inelastic supply, if the price that must be paid for it exceeds what it could earn in other industries, e.g. because minimum wages are fixed by trade unions—the railways used to com-

[1] In this case marginal private cost will exceed marginal social cost, which is based on the price of the factors and not on their marginal cost to the undertaking. It is social cost which is relevant.

plain strongly because their wages were more closely regulated than wages in road transport.

Such producers' surpluses, together with what is available from consumers' surplus, ought certainly to be included in the calculation to decide whether the continued incurring of escapable indivisible costs is justified or not. It is unlikely that they can be made available to the undertaking, but whether they are available or not they ought to be included in the calculation, and precision requires that we should say, not that the sum available from consumers' surplus must cover the indivisible cost, but that that sum must cover the indivisible cost less producers' surpluses accruing to outside factors.

The principle underlying the two-part tariff and simple price discrimination is that those who cannot escape must make the largest contribution to indivisible cost, and that those to whom the commodity does not matter much may escape. The man who has to cross Dupuit's bridge to see his dying father is mulcted thoroughly; the man who wishes only to see the scenery on the other side gets off lightly. The public's attitude to price discrimination is not capable of rational exposition. Broadly speaking, it dislikes discrimination, but special cases are tolerated. Discrimination according to income is accepted from doctors, the government or electricity undertakings, and used to be accepted from shopkeepers, but would now probably be resented if tried by the baker or the bus conductor. On the railways it is freely accepted as between commodities, but not as between different parcels of the same commodity. The law allows a lower charge to be made to a man who has canal transport open to him, but the railways may not discriminate for or against a farmer whose land happens to be more fertile than that of his neighbour.

Where there are escapable indivisible expenses to be covered the case for discrimination is clear. It secures an output nearer the optimum, and levies the indivisible cost on those who get the greatest benefit (measured by their consumers' surplus) from retaining the indivisible resource in this line of production. Moreover, it is possible in some cases that the net result may be that everyone pays a lower price for the commodity than he would if there were no discrimination. This is certain if the undertaking is trying to maximise its net revenue and (but not otherwise) if marginal divisible cost is falling. But it is also possible if the undertaking is out merely to cover its costs and could cover them without discrimination, since reducing the price to some persons with elastic demands may increase the surplus over marginal cost which they contribute, and thus allow the price to others also to be reduced. Nevertheless, discrimination between persons as such is always awkward; discrimination is much easier if impersonal categories can be found which more or less arrange themselves in order of elasticity of demand, such as discrimination between types of traffic, between different uses for electric current, or even discrimination according to income. In what follows we shall speak of an industry charging different prices for different services when we mean charging any user on the basis of some impersonal category prices which yield different surpluses over marginal cost. allowing for the fact that the marginal cost may be different, e.g. the difference in the marginal costs of transporting 20 tons of coal and 20 tons of hay.

If the available consumers' surplus is not by itself enough to meet the indivisible cost, but would do so together with the producers' surplus, the undertaking should be maintained. It will, however, run at a loss unless it is allowed to discriminate between its suppliers. A subsidy is then the only way out, if the optimum allocation of resources is to be maintained, but this is not as good a solution as would be some method that collected the producers' surplus, since those who should pay are those who receive the benefit.

When an industry with escapable indivisible expenses is in competition with another offering similar services, the rules for pricing become more precise. In no case should the price of any service be below the marginal cost of performing it. It may exceed marginal cost if the other industry's marginal cost is higher, but in that case it should not be as high as the marginal cost of the other industry, or the other industry may capture trade to which its marginal cost does not entitle it. An industry then performs services only where its divisible marginal cost is the lower, and collects revenue towards its indivisible expenses only to (not more than) the extent that it can perform the service more cheaply than the other industry.

For two industries to exist it must be the case that each industry performs some services at lower divisible marginal cost than the other; from each of its services it will collect towards its indivisible expenses. The amount of revenue which an industry can so collect however, depends on the margins between its divisible marginal costs for each of its services, and what would be the divisible marginal cost of these services to the other industry if it were performing them.

No problem arises if the surplus each receives is adequate to cover escapable indivisible costs. The interesting problems arise if one or both is unable to do so.

If one can cover its escapable indivisible cost but not the other, the one which cannot ought to be closed down (or not started if the commitment is not yet made). There is only one case which seems to throw doubt on this principle. Take the following simplified assumptions. There are two industries, X and Y, both with indivisible costs, and each offers the same services, a, b, c and d. X has lower marginal costs for a and b, and Y lower marginal costs for c and d. Suppose that there is only one unit of each service, and that the difference between Y's marginal cost and X's marginal cost on c and on d is so great that Y can earn enough surplus on c and d to cover all its escapable indivisible costs, and its future is assured. The problem then turns on a and b. Suppose the cost situation to be as follows, in money units:

	Divisible costs		Indivisible costs	Total
	a	b		
X's costs	1	1	2	4
Y's costs	2	3	already covered	5

If the X industry is maintained it should serve a and b because its marginal costs are lower. As far as competition with Y is concerned, it can extract from a and b prices of just under 2 and 3 respectively, which would yield a surplus of just under 3 and amply cover its indivisible expenses. But suppose that, quite apart from competition, b cannot afford to pay a higher price than 1, while a, in the absence of the alternative service offered by Y, would be willing to pay as much as 4. It may be argued that the correct solution is to keep the X industry going, to charge b only 1, and to charge a 3 but prevent it from transferring to Y, either by legislation or by some arrangement compelling Y to charge more than X. In this way both a and b will be served by X at a total cost (4) lower than if they were both served by Y (5), and anyway if the X industry were not maintained b could not be served at all since it could not afford Y's marginal cost. This is one of the railways' most seductive arguments in the current controversy. The valuable high-rated traffics, it is said, ought to be kept to the railway to contribute towards indivisible expenses to which the low-rated traffics cannot afford to contribute much,[1] and since the railway needs to extract from them more than it would cost to send them by road, some arrangement must be made to prevent road transport from getting them, e.g. compelling road transport to adopt the railway's schedule of charges. It is an attractive fallacy. To return to our example, the argument is really that the service *a*, though it could get itself performed by Y for 2, must pay 3 to X in order that *b* may be carried at a price it can afford, and that this is justifiable because the real value of the service *a* must be at least 3 or it would not be bought at that price. The answer is that in calculating the consumers' surplus on the service *a* performed by X, it is wrong to exclude the possibility of getting the same satisfaction more cheaply from Y; this is as if my consumers' surplus on bread were calculated on the assumption that no potatoes or other foodstuffs were available. Given that the Y industry exists, and offers the service at 2, the maximum consumers' surplus on *a* bought from X is 1, and it would be invalid to charge more just so as to provide resources from which *b* can be served. Alternatively, we can put the argument like this. The Y industry will exist in any case, and can serve *a* at a cost of 2. If therefore the X industry is also maintained, at a total cost of 4, to serve both *a* and *b*, we can say that serving *b* is adding 2 to the total costs that there would be if the X industry were not maintained and *a* were served by Y, and *b* should not be served unless it is willing to pay at least this 2. In no circumstances is it justifiable to make *a* pay more than Y's divisible cost. If anyone considers that *b* is a terribly important service,[2] then by all means subsidise

---

[1] Actually it is doubtful whether the high-rated traffics do in fact contribute more than the low-rated. Receipts per ton mile (cf. *Annual Railway Returns,* 1938) suggest that they do:

		Classes	Classes
	Coal	1–6	7–21
pence per ton mile	1·08	0·96	2·00

But receipts per wagon mile suggest the opposite:

pence per wagon mile	10·51	9·38	5·62

The low-rated traffics have higher marginal costs per wagon mile, but is the difference as great as this?

[2] One of the railway arguments is rather like this. It is important, it says, that the heavy-rated traffics should continue to be carried, and if the other

it sufficiently to make the X industry able to meet its costs—whereupon both *a* and *b* will rightly be served by X—but such a subsidy should come from general taxation; why pick on *a* and compel it to subsidise *b*?

It is also possible that if there is competition between two industries, each with indivisible expenses, neither may be able to pay its way. Consider, on the same assumptions as before, the following cost situation:

	Divisible	Indi- visible	Divisible	Indi- visible	Total
	a	*b*	*c*	*d*	
X's cost	1	1	4	3	3	12
Y's cost	2	3	1	2	5	13

traffics go by road these traffics will have to pay more to the railway, or if they cannot afford to pay enough to keep the railway going, the railway will have to close and the traffics either not be carried or go by road at enormous cost.

Assume first that the consequence would be that the heavy traffics would pay higher rates by rail, enough to maintain the railway. This, the argument runs, is bad, because it raises the prices of raw materials, and secondly because in altering the ratio of transport costs of raw materials to finished products it gives incentives to alter the location of industry. The first argument seems curious; if an alteration in rates structure lowers costs on finished products and raises them on raw materials, the final price is not necessarily affected; indeed, if we assume that the railway remains but cannot retain the finished products in free competition, then the final price is lowered because total transport cost is lowered. The second is true, but not conclusive; the location pattern has grown up on the basis of a distorted rates structure; if now rates are altered, we may get a different location pattern, but it will be just different, not worse—it may be better since it corresponds more to real costs.

If the consequence would be that heavy traffics could not alone maintain the railway, parts of which then had to be closed, and could not then afford the high cost by rail, they cannot be important traffics in any economic sense. But, as argued above, if they are important, let them be subsidised, but out of the general revenues. This applies equally to the contention that the railway should not be allowed to contract because of its usefulness in war. If we must maintain in peace time railway facilities larger than our peace-time need, the Government should subsidise the railways to the necessary extent. Given a subsidy, competition should then be on the basis of the rule that price must be not less than railway marginal cost but not more than the marginal cost of any available alternative form of transport.

If the consequence would be that the railway would contract and the traffics go by road at high cost, no action is necessary. If they can go by road at high cost they could pay the same price to the railway. If that price would not keep the railway alive, then road transport is actually cheaper and the railway ought not to be maintained.

Neither can pay its way if both industries are established. The X industry will secure a and b, but the maximum revenue it can get from them is 5, while it needs 6 to keep alive; and Y will secure c and d, can get only 6, but needs 8. The essence of this situation is that if we take the services for which either of these industries has lower divisible costs, the sum of its divisible and indivisible costs exceeds the divisible costs of the other for those services, so that total costs if there is only one industry must be smaller than if there are two.[1] Consequently, if both industries have indivisible costs and neither can pay when the correct pricing rules are applied, only the one with the lower total costs should be maintained.

The net result may be summed up as follows. Where there are indivisible expenses, price should be not less than marginal cost, but not as much as the marginal cost of competing industries, and the undertaking should not be maintained unless the surplus over divisible costs covers the indivisible expenses. The only exception to this is the case where two industries offer the same services and neither pays if they follow these rules; then only the one with the lower total costs should be retained.

5. The fourth consequence of equating price with escapable cost is that the undertaking's receipts may be greater or less than its expenses. This may happen whenever accounting costs are different from escapable, in the circumstances distinguished in Section I, 5.

If price equals marginal cost, a loss will be made on inescapable expenses unless marginal costs rise until they are equal to the average of all costs, escapable and inescapable. If marginal cost exceeds average cost, there will be a profit. This profit is a rent for the use of some scarce resource owned by the undertaking. For example, suppose that the road system can be extended only at rising marginal cost; then if the government based motor taxation on this marginal cost it would probably receive each year a sum well in excess of its expenditure on the roads. The difference is a rental for the use of existing roads, and is a very proper

---

[1] Take the sum of X's divisible and indivisible costs for a and b as p, and the sum of Y's divisible and indivisible costs for c and d as q. Y's divisible costs for a and b are less than X's divisible and indivisible, say $p - m$, and X's divisible costs for c and d are less than Y's divisible and indivisible, say $q - n$. Then if there are two industries, total costs are $p + q$. But if there is only one industry total costs are either $p + q - n$ if it is X, or $q + p - m$ if it is Y.

and necessary charge if road transport is not to develop beyond the economic point. In what follows it will be assumed that marginal cost is less than average cost, and that prices based on it cover the escapable but not the inescapable costs. The discussion follows the cost categories of Section I, 5.

If there are inescapable expenses due to the fact that some assets do not have to be renewed, the undertaking will show a loss if price covers only escapable cost.

Take first the indivisible permanent assets, whose value outside the undertaking is less than their original cost. Someone has to bear the difference; why should it be the investors? The expenses were undertaken for the benefit of the consumers, and would not have been undertaken unless it was considered that the consumers were willing to pay enough to justify these resources being specialised to their use. There is no reason why the mere fact that the resources have now been specialised should throw the cost on the investors, or on anyone but those consumers for whose benefit the resources have been put into their present form. Non-renewable and renewable indivisible expenses should, in fact, be treated alike, in that they should be a charge on consumers' surplus, distributed over the consumers in whatever way will least reduce demand; the difference is that renewable indivisible expenses are escapable, and that while in their case the undertaking should be discontinued unless they can be fully used, in the case of non-renewable indivisible expenses the undertaking should go on even if what can be extracted from consumers' surplus is not enough to meet the original cost.

Consider next assets which are permanent but divisible, such as the cost of land for transport tracks. Whether they are escapable or not will depend on whether the industry is working to capacity. If it is working to capacity such expenses enter into marginal cost, and no loss is incurred. If it is working below capacity these expenses are uncovered. Part of the capacity is being used, and part is not, but price being equal to marginal cost, neither part is covered. That part which is in excess is due to mistaken investment on the part of the entrepreneur, and it is right that he should bear the loss. But why should not the consumers pay for that part of the capacity which they use? Resources have had to be specialised to meet their convenience, and the fact of excess capacity should not throw the cost on to the investors. The proper course is to write off the cost of such part as is in excess, but to levy on consumers' surplus, according to what the traffic will bear, to cover as much of the original cost of what is used as can be covered. The difference between divisible renewable and divisible unrenewable assets is that the latter will continue to be used whether the levy on consumers' surplus is adequate to cover the cost or not, whereas the former enter into marginal cost.

Assets which are divisible and renewable, but some of which will not be renewed because of a contraction of demand, have already been dealt with. Price should cover the cost of renewal. The result, however, is that that part of the assets which is not to be renewed will earn no amortisation and will show a loss. The loss is due to mistaken foresight and it is right that the entrepreneur should bear it.

An undertaking may also show a loss or a profit because the cost of replacing its assets rises or falls. If replacement cost rises, escapable cost rises, and price rises above original cost. If replacement cost falls, price falls below original cost. These windfall profits and losses are due to mistaken foresight, and properly remain with the entrepreneur.

6. The net conclusion is that, at least in public utility undertakings and state industries, price should not fluctuate irregularly; should cover not only short-run but also long-run marginal cost; not only long-run marginal cost but also, preferably by way of price discrimination, escapable indivisible cost as well; and not only these, but as much of the cost of non-renewable assets as can be extracted from consumers' surplus by price discrimination (but only to the extent to which such assets are actually used). The only losses the undertaking should bear are losses due to mistaken foresight: where the entrepreneur has failed to estimate correctly the level of output, the amount of consumers' surplus available for unrenewable assets, or a change in replacement cost.

III

THE PRINCIPLES OF CO-ORDINATION

1. The first problem in co-ordination is one of terminology. There is an awful confusion in the voluminous literature on this subject because hardly any writers recognise the logical difference between the framework and the principles of co-ordination. It is possible to co-ordinate two industries by private agreement between the undertakings, by nationalisation, by free competition,

by amalgamation, by legislation dividing the traffic, by licensing, or in other ways. No sound judgment can be passed on any of these schemes until one knows what is its purpose—what principles it will operate to secure the correct division of function between the two industries. The first thing to settle is the principle on which co-ordination should be based; discussion of the framework is subsidiary.

2. The economist's principle is escapable social cost; if two industries can perform the same service, one at a lower social cost than the other, the cheaper should perform it, unless the superior quality of the service offered by the other is worth more than the difference in cost—allowing, e.g. for differences of speed in transport, or in the quality of the space heating done by gas and by electricity.

Some proposals have been based on one or other of two other principles. One is that the revenues of established industries should be protected, so that they can pay interest on invested capital. In so far as this means that an industry must meet all escapable costs, divisible and indivisible, it is included in the economist's principle. But in practice it means more than this, and this is the well-known fallacy. This is the principle that has been applied in the restrictive licensing of road transport in this country.[1] The other principle is that it is better for industries to join together to exploit the market than to fight over it, e.g. that road and rail would do better to have a common rate classification which milked the high-valued traffics, and to share them on some arbitrary principle, than by quarrelling to let such traffics pass at low rates. This principle has seemed from time to time to be the one most likely to be adopted but needs no discussion here.

There is, however, one objection to the escapable cost principle which is very widely held, and which deserves some attention. Some people consider that all the services performed by an industry should be taken as a whole, and that it does not matter if the separate parts pay, so long as the whole pays. According to this, some services should be performed at less than marginal cost, and subsidised from profits made on other services, and an industry which tries to do this may be handicapped if some other

[1] For detailed discussion of its application in decided cases see G. J. Ponsonby, "The New Conditions of Entry into the Road Haulage Business," *Economica*, May 1937; D. N. Chester, *Public Control of Road Passenger Transport*, Ch. XI; and G. Walker, *Road and Rail*, Ch. VII.

industry is allowed to charge only marginal cost for the profitable services which were being relied on for subsidy. There are many points in transport where this kind of policy is urged. For example, it is suggested that some traffics should be carried below marginal cost, or some classes of passengers; that profits should be made where the population is dense and used to provide transport facilities where it is sparse; that there should be flat rates not varying with distance, the short-distance traffic subsidising the very long; or that peak travellers should subsidise the off-peak. There are similar arguments for electricity and gas; e.g. that rates should be uniform throughout the country, with the odd difference that in electricity it is the off-peak consumer who is expected to provide the subsidy.

We have already seen that where there are indivisible elements in cost, not all services should contribute equally to total expenses; each should pay its marginal cost plus what it can afford. The proposals under discussion here are proposals for charging less than marginal cost.

There are three objections. The first is that charging less than marginal cost in different areas distorts the economic factors which influence the distribution of the population. Population growth is stimulated in those regions at the expense of other regions. Part of the result is a gift to landlords and earners of quasi-rents, and to this extent the good intentions of those who make this sort of proposal are simply frustrated; but in so far as their intentions succeed, they distort the location pattern. Now it may be that the location pattern ought to be altered in these ways—broadly speaking that more people ought to be encouraged to live in places now sparsely populated, and vice versa. But it is doubtful whether transport and electricity authorities, acting separately, should be left to decide such matters. They do not necessarily take into account all that is relevant, and they may even pursue contradictory policies—the transport authorities may well be charging specially high rates to a region which is able to afford them only because the electricity authorities are charging specially low ones. The decision that some places are to be made more attractive and others less so is for the town and country planning authorities, and it is for them to say whether the penalties and attractions are to be subsidies to transport and electricity or something else.

The second objection is that if such subsidies are to be paid, it does not follow that they should be levied on other consumers of transport or electricity. It may be convenient to subsidise some users of transport by taxing others, but convenience is not the best principle of taxation.

The third objection is that this "over-all" sort of accounting makes difficult the control of the activities of such undertakings. If a manager is told that every service must cover its marginal cost, accounts can be devised which show whether it does or not, and his efficiency judged accordingly. If he is told only that he must cover all his costs it is more difficult to judge his efficiency, since he may be covering up gross errors in some parts of the undertaking simply by exploiting the consumers in some other part. This, in practice, should prove to be one of the most important principles in the administration of State enterprises—that each part of the enterprise must stand on its own feet. No business man would try to run a department store without separate accounts for each department, and the public's problem of checking the efficiency of different parts of an undertaking is not less important.

Nevertheless, to hold that some services should be subsidised is not necessarily inconsistent with accepting cost as the correct principle for co-ordination, since the decision to subsidise still leaves open the question which of two industries should perform the service. If price is below marginal cost it is unlikely that co-ordination will in practice be based on marginal cost, but there is no theoretical difficulty; all that is required is that the different industries should be equally subsidised so that the difference between their prices should equal the difference between their costs. Cost remains the only principle of co-ordination worthy of serious consideration.

3. Given acceptance of the cost principle, one may decide to put it into effect in more or less rough-and-ready ways. For example, if it is thought that costs are cheaper by rail for all traffics travelling more than 50 miles, or weighing more than 30 lbs. per cubic foot, or requiring less than three changes of wagon if sent by rail, one may issue instructions based on one or more of these principles—in some countries this is the basis of the road-rail legislation. Obviously this is a very distant approach to the cost principle, and most traders in this country would feel that co-ordination here should get beyond such generalisations to more exact consideration of costs for each type of transaction.

4. The nearest approximation to the cost principle is to quote

a price for each separate transaction, based on the cost of each separate transaction, and to use the services of whichever industry is cheaper. These prices may be actual or notional; that is to say, co-ordination may proceed by quoting real prices to the buyer, and letting him choose; or by reserving the choice to the management which then acts on the basis of its own calculations of which would be the cheaper. In practice in this country, for gas and electricity and for road and rail transport, the decision must be left to the buyer. In the case of gas and electricity, no one has ever contemplated leaving it to a fuel overseer to decide which each consumer must use. In the case of transport, some persons have suggested it, but the suggestion is not likely to be accepted. Traders' organisations have always insisted unanimously on freedom of choice between different forms of transport. Some advocates of nationalisation have thought otherwise, but not all; for instance, the Trades Union Congress in its recent report,[1] while paying lip service to managerial decision as an ultimate aim, provides for separate bodies to run road and rail transport, and not, as would otherwise be necessary, for a single manager to operate at each receiving point and decide which form of transport is to be used. Traders value the right to make their own choice because there are so many variables in the quality of transport service, and it is unlikely that any Government will wish to force any other solution on them. Co-ordination must occur through the buyer choosing on the basis of prices which reflect costs.

Exact reflection, we have already seen, has its disadvantages, and they are likely to prove overwhelming. Prices will have to be based on long-run marginal costs rather than short-run; and they must not fluctuate irregularly. Gas and electricity prices already follow these precepts; road transport rates, however, do not and must be brought into line. Most people, including the traders, agree that there should be a codified road rates structure. Admittedly this is not easy to draw up, but it is not more difficult than the codification of railway rates, which has existed for more than fifty years. The main disagreement on this issue has been not whether there should be a code, but on the acceptance of cost as the correct principle for such a code.

We may now consider our two cases in greater detail.

5. The principal practical difficulty in co-ordinating gas and electricity on the cost principle is that presented by the daily peak.

[1] T.U.C., *The Public Operation of Transport*, 1945.

Here the electricity industry is the victim of its history. At its start, electricity was used mainly for lighting, and cheaper rates were offered, correctly based on long-run marginal cost, to stimulate consumption during the day for other purposes. These succeeded so well that in many undertakings the peak has shifted from the evening to the day.[1] Rates have not, however, been properly adjusted to take account of this change. This is partly because rates are sticky, partly because of the technical difficulty which used to exist (now more or less solved) of recording consumption according to the time of day, and partly because of the widespread adoption of the two-part tariff.

The two-part tariff has solid advantages; customer costs, which do not vary with consumption, can be put into the fixed charge, and so can the consumer's contribution to indivisible expenses adjusted to his capacity to pay. Its great disadvantage, however, is that in encouraging customers to use as wide a range of electrical appliances as possible, it does not discriminate between those which come on to the peak and those which do not. The result, according to a recent calculation,[2] is that some of the more expensive forms of consumption barely cover their marginal cost, if that, and make no contribution to indivisible expenses. In the gas industry, which has not so acute a peak problem, as gas can be stored (though distribution costs are effected), the two-part tariff would not have this disadvantage, yet for historical reasons the two-part tariff is much less common here.

The electricity industry has a choice between three solutions. One is to have separate wiring of different types of consumption which occur at different times and are separately recorded. This is done in some cases, e.g. for large commercial water heaters

[1] In some undertakings the position is uncertain and periods during which the peak may occur now cover a large part of the day. Cost allocation becomes a ticklish business when there is a shifting peak. A sub-committee of the Electrical Research Association has studied the problem in a report entitled, *An Improved Method for Allocating to Classes of Consumers the Demand Related Portion of the Standing cost of Electricity Supply*, 1945. The suggested solution is to allocate the full maximum demand charge to all loads whose maximum demand is known to coincide with the station peak, and to allocate to others by a formula taking both their maximum demands and their consumption during the potential peak period into account, on the theory that a load with a high load factor is likely to affect the peak more than a load with a low load factor.

[2] Report by the Fuel and Power Advisory Council, *Domestic Fuel Policy*, Cmd. 6762, 1946.

charged only at night; but it would be too expensive to apply to the domestic consumer. The second alternative is to have meters which record peak and off-peak consumption separately. These are unpopular in the industry partly because of their cost (which would probably fall if they were demanded in large numbers), partly because of a sort of conservatism which accepts charging different prices for different uses but resists the idea of a price difference based on time, and partly because they might have to be complicated to meet the needs of undertakings whose peaks are imminently liable to shift in incidence. The third possibility, and the easiest to bring into effect, would be to vary the fixed charge according to the appliances used by the consumer, so that a man who used a fire would pay more than a man who used only lamps, and a man who had an electric cooker still more, the difference depending on the extent to which the appliance is likely to increase the size of the peak. The difficulty in applying this is the difficulty of checking the number of appliances the consumer is using and detecting secret appliances, but this is not so difficult as it sounds since it is possible to guess roughly from the consumption shown by the meter whether the consumer is likely to have more appliances than he admits to or not; this makes detection much easier than the Postmaster General's problem of detecting those who forget to buy a wireless licence.

6. In transport the principal problem in basing price on cost is the cost of the tracks.

If the cost of the tracks used by road and rail were independent of the traffic each carried, the solution would be simple; their costs would not be part of marginal cost, and should not enter into prices in such a way as to divert traffic from one to the other. The solution advocated by Brigadier-General Sir Osborne Mance[1] is of this kind; he proposes that the Government take over financial responsibility for railway tracks and roads, leaving road and rail to compete on the basis of other costs. The validity of this solution depends on the assumption that total track costs would not be affected if as a result some traffics were diverted from one system to the other. Now this is a question of fact to be determined by the Government. General Mance first made this proposal for East Africa, where it is clearly arguable that the Government would have to maintain both a railway and a road net the sizes of which would not be much affected by any likely traffic changes in the

[1] H. O. Mance, *The Road and Rail Transport Problem*, 1940.

near future. In this country the best reasons for considering that the position may be similar are the argument that the size of the road system is determined mainly by the number of private cars travelling on bank holidays, and that the number of commercial vehicles, which are more closely competitive with the railways, has little effect on road costs; and the military case for maintaining larger road and rail networks than are required in peace time. If these arguments add up to the conclusion that expenditure on road and rail tracks is largely independent of competition between road and rail, then it ought certainly not to be taken into account in that competition.

This decision has to be made by those who know the relevant facts, in this case the Government. In countries where it is decided that track expenditure depends on whether traffic goes by road or by rail, such expenditure is part of the marginal costs of traffic, and should be reflected in prices.[1] This is where non-renewable expenditure presents difficulty. To extend their facilities, both road and rail have to purchase land and put it into suitable form for tracks. This expense is a part of marginal cost, so long as the system is not working below capacity. A great battle has raged over the issue whether road transport should pay enough to cover the interest on all past investment of this kind. The railways are expected to pay such interest, if they can, and claim that it is unfair that road transport should get a "legacy from the past" which they cannot share. Their contention would be the nonsense which economists have usually asserted it to be if there were excess capacity in roads as there is in railways. But there is not. Every extension of the road system involves heavy expenditure on land and conversion, and the charge made to road transport should be at a rate which covers this. If it is at such a rate we can be pretty sure that it will be adequate to pay interest on the entire network of roads, assuming constant marginal cost, and much more than this if we assume that extending the road network takes place at rising marginal cost. Some economists have argued that road transport ought to pay only a sum equal to the annual

[1] Most of the proposals for "putting road and rail on an equal basis in respect of track costs" violate this principle. Such are: (a) that the Government should meet the cost of all tracks out of taxation; (b) that the Government should own all tracks and charge vehicles, whether road or rail, *the same* ton-mile rate for use of the tracks; (c) that road transport should pay in taxes a total sum equal to the cost of railway tracks. Equality of charge is economic only if there is equality of cost.

expenditure on the roads, but this is not so. Given constant marginal cost, road transport ought to pay on existing roads not only their maintenance but also interest, and given rising marginal cost it should pay also a rent. The railways have reached what is probably a true conclusion via an invalid argument.

Let us suppose, however, that it is not the case that there are rising marginal costs in extending the road net, and that to charge marginal cost would leave an indivisible cost uncovered. The indivisible expenditure is divided into the escapable (renewable) and the inescapable (which is not shown in current road finance, but for which items appear in railway accounts). Each system must cover its escapable indivisible expenditure separately, out of consumers' surplus. Since the traffics in which each system is superior will be different, those goods which make a high contribution to the indivisible costs of the railway will make none to road costs and vice versa. Each system will have a rates structure, but these structures will not be similar, as is so often proposed, but opposites. The high-rated traffics of road transport will be the low-rated traffics of the railway, and vice versa.

Assuming that the Government owns the road (or the railway track) but not the vehicle, how should it charge the users of the track? That part of the cost of the road which varies with use should enter into marginal cost. This happens automatically if it is levied as a tax on petrol (or coal) or some other index or record of vehicle miles run.[1] To some extent, however, cost varies with the number of vehicles rather than the miles they run, because the roads have to be wide and numerous enough to take the maximum number of vehicles wanting to run, and on bank holidays they are nearly all out; to this extent the tax should be on the vehicle, irrespective of mileage. Theoretically one should separate out these two sources of variation in costs, as the electric undertakings separate out standing from running costs, and set the fixed and variable taxes accordingly; but in practice exact division is probably not very important.

The escapable indivisible part of the track cost is more difficult. This must not enter into marginal cost, and should therefore definitely not be recovered by a tax on fuel or on the vehicle. The correct solution is that when rates are being fixed a sum should

---

[1] There are crucial problems here in deciding which classes of vehicle do most damage; see Ministry of Transport (Salter), *Report of the Conference on Road and Rail Transport*, 1932.

be added to all rates that can bear it, in so far as they can; carriers (including persons carrying on their own account) should then make regular declarations of what they have carried, and pay the appropriate tolls—just as cinemas collect and pay over entertainment duty. (This filling of a large gap in our statistics of transport would in any case be very valuable.) There would doubtless be some attempts to defraud, but if the ultimate penalty were loss of licence, evasion would probably not be very great. In any case, the problem arises only to the extent to which transport remains in private ownership. In a nationalised transport system the appropriate tolls would be added to prices and the rest would be mere book work. (It should be remembered that we are assuming that marginal cost of the track is less than average cost: if it is not none of this arises as the indivisible expenses are covered simply by charging marginal cost.)

There remain the inescapable costs to which the owners of the track are entitled in so far as they can get them from the users. Strictly, each system should be treated separately, the railway getting what it can from its traffics, and road authorities the same. General Mance, who believes that more or less all railway and road track expenses are inescapable, has suggested that they should be pooled, so that in effect goods going by rail might contribute towards the maintenance of roads, and vice versa. If railway traffics cannot yield from their consumers' surplus enough to cover inescapable expenses, the loss has to be borne somewhere. At present the shareholders bear it; and if the Government owned the tracks and found itself in a similar position, the Government would bear it for railways as it does for roads (no interest charge is recorded on past investments in roads). If the Government has to bear a loss, it will levy taxes on the community. There is no obvious reason why it should levy specially on traffic going by one system to meet losses on another; this might or might not prove the most convenient source of revenue, but convenience is only one of the canons of taxation.

One of the difficult problems is the difference between different tracks. Not only are some roads less expensive to build than others per mile, but the density of traffic varies from one to another, and if rates were the same some would make profits and others losses. The railway companies get over this by charging exceptional rates on routes with high traffic density, and the co-existence side by side of two competing systems, road and rail, applying different principles, must have caused some uneconomic diversion of traffic in the past. A nationalised road transport industry could be brought into line with railway practice, its ton-mile rates varying with traffic densities on the routes to be used. But the problem is soluble even if road transport is not nationalised, on lines already suggested. If road rates are codified, the rate including a toll to be paid over to the Government at regular intervals, the amount of the toll can be adjusted to traffic density, traffics passing between some places paying lower tolls than others. A road rates code would in any case have to take account of density, back loads, and the other matters which distinguish one route from another, so this would not be a new principle. However, a Government seeking to avoid complications might decide that the simplest thing was to have a uniform rate throughout the country. If it did, co-ordination of road and rail would be upset unless the railways were put on the same basis. From the point of view of co-ordination it does not matter much which basis is adopted; what matters is that road and rail tracks should both be paid for on the same principles.

It will be obvious that the co-ordination of road and rail on the basis of cost is no simple matter. All the work of determining in actual figures what part of track costs varies with traffic, and what part is indivisible but escapable, remains to be done, also the task of allocating these costs properly to traffics on the basis of what they will bear, taking into account the limits set to each system's charge by the marginal cost of the other. The calculations involved may lead some to conclude that it would be too costly to try to co-ordinate on the basis of cost, but once it is recognised that at best only broad approximations will be possible, the work can be kept within reasonable limits, especially as it is the initial allocations that are difficult, and the year-to-year changes are small. Only the Government possesses the information on which to base the allocations; all that outsiders can do is to set out what seem to be the logical categories.

IV

THE FRAMEWORK OF CO-ORDINATION

1. The principle that co-ordination should be based on cost is independent of the framework adopted to secure co-ordination. In this country four methods have been considered, (1) free price competition, (2) restrictive licensing, (3) private agreement, and (4) amalgamation, including nationalisation.

2. The first problem which free competition presents is co-ordination in the building of road and rail tracks. We have seen, in Section II, 4 that, given two industries with indivisibilities, price competition between them can secure proper co-ordination. If, however, the facilities are not given, or questions of extending them arise, competition between indivisible elements does not work smoothly. If, for example, a railway company is contemplating laying a new track, whether this should be done or not will depend to some extent on whether the road authorities propose to build parallel and/or feeder roads. Such uncertainties hold up development; they have, for instance, been one of the obstacles to the electrification of the railways. If the sums of money involved were small, and development could proceed a little at a time, the competitive process would adjust the facilities provided by competing industries. But where the sums are so large and indivisible, under-development through uncertainty on the one hand, or over-development through ignorance of rival proposals on the other, can best be avoided by consultation. The network of railway tracks and of roads should be planned as a whole, following the principle elucidated in Section II, 4, that both should be provided, in competition with each other, where with price discrimination both would pay, but that only one should be provided if only one by itself would pay.

Now the present situation in this country is particularly anomalous because, not only are road authorities separate from the railway track authorities, but roads are provided in competition with railway tracks without the authorities having to consider whether these roads earn their cost or not. Road and rail track building should clearly be done at least in consultation; and would probably be done best if there were a single authority, i.e. if the Government nationalised the railway tracks and planned road and rail tracks together. Nationalisation of railway vehicles and operation does not, of course, follow from the nationalisation of the tracks, and it has often been proposed that the one should be done without the other. In what follows we shall assume that road and rail tracks are commonly owned by the Government, which charges rail and road vehicle operators for their use. What we shall discuss is the co-ordination of the service provided by such operators, in terms of the choice between free competition, licensing, and amalgamation, including nationalisation.

3. Free price competition could secure a very precise co-

ordination, based on hour-to-hour changes in cost. To achieve it, road and rail would have to be placed on an equal footing; the railways relieved of their obligations to carry and given freedom to vary their rates at will, and road transport freed from restrictive licensing. This is generally admitted. What has not been generally accepted, although the railways have always pressed the point strongly, is that it would involve a revolution in the treatment of road costs, both in deciding what was to be levied, and in deciding how it was to be levied, and to the extent to which there may be escapable indivisible elements in road costs it would require road rates to be put on to a what-the-traffic-would-bear basis. In the light of all this, no one can pretend that the competition between road and rail in pre-war years was either fair or based on cost, or that the resulting traffic diversions were not to some extent un-economic in the social sense. However, given the necessary adjustments, free price competition based on cost could certainly achieve a proper co-ordination.

The disadvantages we have already seen. Since rates would be based not on long-run but on short-run marginal cost, the railways, which suffer from excess capacity, would have difficulty in earning amortisation quotas on that part of their investment which requires renewal, though perhaps this would not be so great a problem if the tracks were disintegrated, since the excess capacity lies there rather than in railway operation. In any case, rates would fluctuate freely from hour to hour, and there would be opportunities for personal discrimination. There are not many persons who feel that the advantage of full hour-to-hour utilisation of resources is great enough to outweigh these disadvantages.

A more limited competition would be possible if both road and rail had their rates fixed by a tribunal on the basis of long-run escapable cost, ironing out fluctuations. It would then be necessary to prevent departures from these rates, and to impose common carrier obligations on both. Charging less than the minimum would be difficult to detect, but could be controlled by making the ultimate penalty forfeiture of licence; no great difficulty seems to be expected in enforcing the minimum road rates now widely proposed.

4. Restrictive licensing does not make any clear contribution towards co-ordination on the basis of cost. For it to be helpful, one must be able to assume that the cost situation demands that there should be fewer road vehicles, and to hope that those which are

licensed will concentrate on the traffics where their marginal costs really are lower than the marginal costs of rail transport. The latter effect will be attained only if road and rail rates correctly reflect the respective costs, and if it is possible for them to do this there is no need for restrictive licensing. In practice there is no pretence in this country that the licensing of road vehicles is based on cost; the avowed object of the Commissioners is to protect the revenues of existing undertakings.

Restrictive licensing of public contractors but not of traders carrying on their own account, and of public passenger vehicles but not of private cars, is obviously uneconomic. It has led to a great expansion of private transport at the expense of public transport, though the latter is more economic. All road transport should be restricted or none. Moreover, if the number of vehicles is restricted below the profitable number, those who get licences are given a semi-monopolistic position which at once reflects itself in the licence acquiring a money value. Why should this gift be presented to operators? If licences are to be restricted they should be sold. But exactly the same results would be achieved by increasing the level of road taxation. The basic problem in coordination is to make road taxation reflect road costs, and if this is done restrictive licensing is unnecessary.

5. Road and rail interests could by private agreement create and maintain rate structures which were based on cost principles. Agreement has been reached on having a road rates structure, but there is no evidence that it is to be based on cost. The interest of the railways is to protect their revenues, and the joint interest of road and rail is to adopt a common classification which enables both to milk the most profitable traffics, sharing the proceeds on some agreed basis. As we have seen, road and rail rates structures should be opposites, in the sense that the goods profitable to the one should be unprofitable to the other; no other structure achieves co-ordination on a cost basis.

6. Some amalgamation has taken place through railway purchase of road undertakings, but the process is likely to be completed by the nationalisation of road and rail transport which has now been announced.

It is not proposed, and is not likely, that road and rail will be fused in the sense that at each point of contact with the public one man will be responsible for both. Separate organisations will be maintained, fusing only at the top. The choice between road and rail will therefore be left to the public. There may be crude attempts to confine it by regulations requiring some traffics to go by rail, e.g. long-distance or heavy traffics, but no such crude approximation to cost is either necessary or a necessary part of nationalisation. There is no reason why the nationalised undertakings should not fix their prices to reflect costs and just let the public make its own choice.

The danger of a nationalised service is its inheritance. It is partly that the Government inherits twenty years of legislation hostile to road transport and a "Whitehall climate" that demands the protection of railway revenues. It is still more the fact that the Government is almost certain to have to pay for the railways more than the railways will be able to earn unless they are bolstered up by restricting road transport. A Government under an obligation to make its railway accounts balance would probably be foolish enough to restrict other forms of transport. This must have wide repercussions. If publicly owned road transport is restricted, either in quantity or by charging prices exceeding costs, the citizens will operate vehicles on their own account under "C" licence, and we shall see continued that uneconomic expansion of traders' transport at the expense of public transport which the licensing system produced before the war. This will threaten the nationalised system, reducing its traffic and profits, and sooner or later the Government will find itself wanting to place restrictions on the right of traders to carry for themselves.

The way out of this is to begin by writing off boldly the excess of the amount which has to be paid to the railway shareholders, so that the nationalised service may start without that burden of over-capitalisation which the L.P.T.B. has to carry. Put on to the books of the new undertaking no more than it can be expected to meet, on its own merits. That would leave the Government free to deal with road transport on its own merits. Most of the apparent case for nationalisation of road transport would vanish. The case for nationalising the railways is presumably that there are notable economies of scale, and that such large concentrations of economic power should be under full public control (though these economies are associated with the tracks rather than with vehicle operation; if the tracks are nationalised there may even be a case for more regional disintegration of vehicle operation, whether this also is nationalised or not). No such argument applies to road transport, and nationalising road transport may merely impart a bureaucratic inefficiency to an industry that might remain more flexible if left to operate on a small scale. The best case for nationalising road transport is that if the railways are nationalised at too high a price, they can be made to pay only by restricting road transport. This best case is a bad one anyway; and would disappear if the water in the price to be paid for the railways were written off immediately.

CHAPTER II

THE TWO-PART TARIFF

The essence of two-part charging is that the consumer is required to pay two charges, one which varies directly with the amount of the commodity consumed, and another which does not. Thus the Post Office charges for the use of the telephone (1) a quarterly rental, payable whether any calls are made or not, plus (2) a charge for each call. Similarly for electricity one may be asked to pay a fixed charge depending on e.g. the size or rateable value of one's house, plus a charge per unit of actual consumption.

This system of charging has made steady progress in this country since it was first suggested in the later years of the nineteenth century. In the electricity industry, where it was first adopted, the two-part tariff is now almost universal; it has been adopted by the Central Electricity Board, which controls wholesale distribution, and strongly recommended to retail distributors by two committees reporting to the Electricity Commissioners. In 1921 it was applied to the telephone system, where it is now the principal method of pricing. Gas legislation has been specially altered to permit undertakings to use the system, and they were adopting it with some zeal in the years immediately preceding the outbreak of war. In industry at least one well-known concern has been using the system for some forty years. Yet, despite this progress the principles of two-part charging are not widely known or understood, and it is the purpose of this essay to elucidate them.

First we shall examine the incentives to two-part charging, and then we shall enquire how it serves the public interest.

There are five possible incentives to two-part charging. First, where in consequence of periodical fluctuations in demand there are regular periods when equipment is standing idle, it is often suggested that the only "scientific" way to allocate costs to consumers is to use a two-part tariff. Secondly, even where there are no such fluctuations regularly foreseeable, an entrepreneur with fixed costs may find it profitable to use a two-part tariff in order to escape the risks of unforeseeable change. Thirdly, the two-part tariff may enable an entrepreneur to extract more revenue from his customers, in given demand conditions, than would a single pricing system. Fourthly, it is a form of price discrimination. And fifthly, it is very appropriate where "customer costs" are large. We shall examine each of these in turn.

I

THE ANALYSIS OF THE PEAK

Most industries are subject to some degree of regular fluctuation in the demand for their products; at some times business is brisk, at others it is slack. The cycle may be diurnal—restaurants, buses and shops have regularly each day hours of peak demand and hours almost of idleness—or it may be weekly, or seasonal, or like the trade cycle it may extend over several years. Where the product can easily be stored, these fluctuations in demand need not induce similar fluctuations in production; the plant can work continuously throughout the year, storing in the slack period the excess output which will be required at the peak. If the product cannot be stored, or the cost of storing is prohibitive, the result is different; the plant must be large enough to meet the maximum demand, and when demand slackens equipment lies idle.

If the idle hours are all needed by the plant for overhauling, repairs or rest, there is no real off-peak excess capacity, and no special problem of peak costing. Again, if we are dealing with equipment which wears out proportionately with use, there is no problem. The cost of the equipment enters directly into marginal cost, which is therefore the same for all units of output. Our problem is best isolated by assuming that the equipment will have to be scrapped on account of technical obsolescence long before it has worn out, and that there is no element of user cost entering into the marginal cost of production. It is also further simplified by assuming that prime costs of operation are zero, so that we may concentrate all attention on the capital costs.

A diagram may help. Fig. 1 shows the number of units consumed at different hours of the day, time being measured on the horizontal and quantity on the vertical axis. It is assumed that consumers take a quantity of one unit marked A throughout the day, a quantity of one unit per hour marked B for four hours, and a quantity of three units per hour marked C for a later four hours. Since the product cannot be stored there must be a total capacity of four units per hour, equal to 96 units a day. Since, however, only 40 units are consumed, there will be 56 units of unused capacity. The problem is now to allocate costs between A, B and C.

Many solutions have been suggested. The simplest is to treat all units of demand alike, dividing the total cost by 40. Assuming that the daily cost of the capital required to produce one unit per hour throughout the day is £24, and that capital costs are constant so that the daily cost of the four units installed is £96, then cost per unit of capacity used is £96 ÷ 40, i.e. £2·4 per hour. Another solution makes each hour of the day contribute the same amount, irrespective of capacity used. The amount required for four units installed is £4 per hour. So, following Fig. 1, for the first five hours

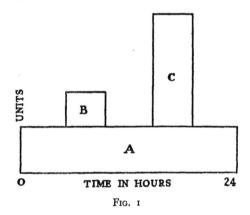

FIG. 1

A is charged £4 per unit per hour; in the next five hours A and B each pay £2 per unit per hour; then A pays £4 per unit per hour; and then A and C pay £1 per unit per hour. In a third solution each piece of equipment used must earn its £24 a day. The first unit supplies A throughout the day and charges £1 per unit. The next supplies B for four hours and C for four hours, and charges £3 per unit per hour. The other two supply C for four hours and charge £6 per unit per hour.

These three are only a small selection from the wide variety of published solutions which is already at our disposal.[1] There is, in fact, hardly any limit to the number of plausible solutions that can be suggested. Equity, from which they mostly start, will

[1] A very useful summary and classification of the published solutions is the monograph by P. Schiller, *Methods of Allocating to Classes of Consumers or Load the Demand-Related Portion of the Standing Costs of Electricity*, published by the British Electrical and Allied Industries Research Association.

support anything. For example, the first solution can be supported on the ground that it is equitable to charge the same price for all units; the second on the ground that it is equitable to make each hour's customers pay for the amortisation of the equipment during that hour, irrespective of how much they use it; and the third on the ground that it is equitable to charge the full cost of each unit of equipment to those who use it. In this field equity is the mother of confusion.

Economists are interested not in equity but in costs. They are predisposed to the view that the most equitable charge is that which corresponds to cost, but their first business is not charges but costs. Economic cost is concerned with the value of resources in alternative uses; it is measured by asking how total expenditure is affected by increasing or by reducing output. Cost is therefore a function of change. It can be found only by enquiring how expenditure is altered if output is altered. Once we start from this point only one solution is possible, that which corresponds to the facts of change, and all others must be rejected.

In terms of the case in hand, the undertaking must compute its costs by asking how its expenditure is affected if demand alters; e.g. if it is asked to supply an extra unit of product. A little reflection will show that the question cannot be answered unless the hour at which the extra unit is to be taken is specified. If it is to be taken at the peak, when the plant is already fully utilised, new plant must be installed, and cost is high. If it is to be taken other than at the peak it may be possible to supply using existing idle equipment, and without extra cost. Peak and off-peak marginal costs are different.

In the early days of electricity supply the problem was simple. The plant was used mainly for lighting purposes, at night, and lay idle during the day. The peak period was clearly definable, and sharply marked off from the off-peak. The cost analysis was simple. Extra supplies at the peak involved additional equipment, and extra off-peak supplies involved none. The whole cost was chargeable to peak supplies, and the cost of off-peak supplies was zero.

This simplicity disappeared when a second peak began to develop. Basing their prices on the cost analysis, undertakings had sold off-peak supplies at very low rates. These had stimulated the demand for electricity for purposes other than lighting, and the consumption for these uses grew steadily until in many undertakings the peak situation altered. In some the morning demand came to exceed evening demand. In others they were about equal. This change created great confusion. When there were two peaks should costs be divided equally between them? If the morning peak exceeded the evening peak should the latter now be disregarded and all costs now be loaded on to the morning peak? Such dramatic changes in price policy were bound to provoke protests, and how should these protests be answered?

The correct policy emerges only if we put the problem into its correct analytical framework. What we are dealing with here is the general problem of amortisation. When an entrepreneur is installing plant, he looks forward through the years and knows that its output will fluctuate with demand. In some years (days or hours) it will be very great, in others small. He cannot allocate the cost of the plant individually between the hours; he hopes only that the profits of all hours taken together will cover the total cost. If we treat the output of each hour as a separate product, the result is exactly as if he were engaged in joint production. The theory of amortisation is a part of the theory of joint costs, and if we take the classical joint cost example of cotton production it helps us to understand the analysis of the peak.

Suppose to begin with that there is no demand for cotton seed whatever; it follows that the whole cost of the plant must be recouped from the sale of lint. Then suppose that there springs up a demand for seed which increases steadily. At first the quantity of seed already being produced in consequence of the demand for lint will exceed the demand for seed. In a competitive market the seed will be sold at a price which only just covers the special costs of recovering it, which for convenience let us assume to be zero. Despite the fact that some seed is being sold, the entire cost of cultivation falls to be contributed by lint; and this must be so as long as the demand for seed at a zero price does not exceed the quantity being produced in consequence of the demand for lint. This corresponds to the simplest peak situation, where there is only one clearly defined peak. The whole cost is attributable to it.

Now let us continue. As the demand for seed grows there comes a point where at zero price the demand just equals the supply available. At that point there ceases to be excess capacity in producing seed. If the demand continues to increase, we can no longer attribute the entire cost of the plant to lint. In a competitive market the price of seed will rise and the price of lint simultaneously fall; the contribution of each to costs will depend solely on demand. In terms of electricity this means that when the morning demand reaches equality with the evening demand, and threatens to exceed it, the proper policy is to raise the morning price and lower the evening price, in an effort to keep the two peaks of equal height. As with lint and seed, the appropriate relation between prices is that which disposes fully of both outputs, eliminating excess capacity. No dramatic price change is called for; the whole cost is not suddenly to be transferred from one peak to the other. As the morning demand grows, the price is raised against it; not at the start to equality with the evening price, but only to such extent as will keep its growth in check, and in line with that of the evening demand, whose further growth is now stimulated by correspondingly reducing its price. If new plant is installed, at this stage, the effort must be to keep it occupied morning and evening, and the appropriate charges are those which secure this result.

But suppose that the morning demand refuses to be kept in check even with this treatment. Let us return to our cotton example. In the situation that we left all the lint and all the seed were finding a market. Now suppose that the demand for seed continues to increase, the seed price rising and the lint price falling. There will come a point where the price of lint falls to zero because the amount of lint produced to satisfy the demand for seed exceeds the demand for lint. At that point and thenceforward the price of seed must cover the whole cost of the plant. There are three stages to the process; a stage where the whole cost is attributable to lint, a stage where the whole cost is attributable to seed, and an intermediate stage where cost allocation depends on demand.

The fact that there is this intermediate stage is usually ignored, but it solves all the problems. Every effort should be made to keep within it, i.e. to keep morning and evening peaks equal. It is only if one demand is so much more powerful than the other that even a zero price for the other cannot equate them that we are in a true peak and off-peak situation where all the cost must be allocated to the peak and none to the off-peak.

Now in practice it is seldom possible to make frequent changes in public utility prices, and so in changing conditions prices cannot be adjusted constantly to the appropriate levels. The main

D

error has been to base prices on the current situation instead of on estimates of future demands. For example, a particular type of electricity load may now be small and definitely off-peak. But if the undertaking charges a very low price based on the existence of excess capacity, and works up the load, it may well grow so enormously as to convert off-peak into peak, as power loads have done. In quoting a price, therefore, the undertaking must have its eye on future possibilities, and not just on present circumstances, and must try to find a mean between a price so high that the load remains altogether undeveloped, and a price so low that a peak emerges—at any rate until such time as the next change in prices becomes feasible.

II

THE PEAK AND THE TWO-PART TARIFF

The home of the two-part tariff is electricity supply. There it was applied long before the peak became a complex problem. In the early days electricity was used primarily for lighting, and the peak was single and clearly defined. Large demands were made on the plant in the evening, while during the day most of the equipment lay idle.

The suggestion that in these conditions the appropriate method of charging is to use a two-part tariff we owe to an English engineer, Dr. John Hopkinson, who became consulting engineer to the first Edison electric power stations in this country, and subsequently Professor of Electrical Engineering at King's College, London. For his presidential address to the Junior Engineering Society in 1892 he chose as subject "The Cost of Electric Supply."[1] The paper begins by stressing the fact that costs are determined by peak demand, goes on to analyse the various elements of fixed and variable cost, and concludes:

> "The ideal method of charge then is a fixed charge per quarter proportioned to the greatest rate of supply the consumer will ever take, and a charge by meter for the actual consumption."[2]

According to this principle it is necessary to discover for each consumer not only how much he consumes during the quarter,

[1] First published in the *Transactions* of the Society, Vol. III. Reprinted with other papers by Hopkinson in his *Original Papers*, Vol. I.

[2] *Original Papers*, p. 261.

but also what is his maximum rate of consumption, defined as the largest amount taken in any small period, e.g. half an hour. Since the equipment of the concern depends on its maximum output in a short period, the consumer is made to pay a fixed charge depending on his maximum in a short period. A similar idea underlies the "Wright" rates offered by some concerns—a type of quantity discount whose gradations depend upon the maximum rate of consumption of the individual consumer.

This conclusion was hailed as a great discovery, and made the basis of many tariffs. Unfortunately it was based on a simple confusion. It is true that it costs a station more to supply 1,000 units if they are all to be taken in one minute than if they are to be spread over a longer period; but this applies to the aggregate output of the station, and not to supplies to the individual consumer. What is true of the individual consumer is that the cost of selling to him is greater if he buys during peak periods than if he buys during slack periods (unless there is excess capacity even at the peak). If therefore he takes 24 units all in one minute during the slack period it may cost less to supply him than if he takes 24 units at the rate of one unit per hour, because in the latter case he adds to capital costs at the peak. The maximum rate at which the individual consumer takes is irrelevant; what matters is how much he is taking at the time of the station's peak.

This point is now generally accepted among the better writers on the subject, but it is not yet fully realised in tariff making. Thus a recent survey of the tariffs of the larger electricity undertakings show 34 per cent offering to industrial consumers two-part tariffs based on individual maximum demand, and a smaller percentage offering such tariffs to domestic consumers.[1] They have also been recommended by a committee reporting to the Electricity Commissioners,[2] and adopted by the Central Electricity Board. Gas engineers, indeed, have gone so far as to suggest for their product two fixed charges based on individual maximum demand, one to take account of the production peak, and one for the distribution peak. Since gas can be stored, the two peaks do not coincide. The volume of output produced varies not from hour to hour, but from season to season, the size of the plant being determined by the greatest demand in any 24 hours. But the

[1] D. J. Bolton, *Costs and Tariffs in Electricity Supply* (1938), pp. 117 and 136.
[2] *Report on Uniformity of Electricity Charges and Tariffs*, by a Committee appointed by the Electricity Commissioners (1930), paras. 119, 136.

calls on the distribution system vary from hour to hour. Two fixed charges to cover the standing costs of production and distribution, a third to cover "customer" costs (discussed in Section IV of this paper), and a variable to cover prime costs, would give the industry a four-part tariff—such are the heights to which this sort of analysis leads!

Hopkinson himself seems to have been a little uneasy about all this, for he added:

> "In fixing the rates of fixed charge it must not be forgotten that it is improbable that all consumers will demand the maximum supply at the same moment, and consequently the fixed charge named might be reduced or some profit be obtained from it."[1]

This, however, merely added to the confusion. For subsequent writers professed to meet the difficulty by introducing the concept of the "diversity factor." Since all consumers are not taking at their maximum rates at the same time, the sum of the individual maximum demands is greater than the total demand on the station at the time of its peak. The diversity factor is defined as the ratio of the sum of the individual demands to the total demand at the time of the peak. There are many theories as to the way in which this diversity factor should be used to "correct" cost allocations based on individual maximum demand; the subject has a vast literature. The latest English work on the subject, D. J. Bolton's *Costs and Tariffs in Electricity Supply* (1938), contains a thirty-page chapter on the diversity factor, full of mathematical symbols, curves and principles deduced from the laws of probability, though from the tentativeness with which he puts them forward, the author himself does not seem to have much faith in them. This is as well, for no amount of correction can alter the fact that the standing costs of the undertaking are related not to the maximum rate at which the individual consumer takes, but to the amount he takes at the time of the station peak. Both the Hopkinson two-part tariff and the Wright quantity discount, based on the maximum demand of the individual consumer, are fallacious in so far as they claim to be exactly allocating to each consumer the costs he causes the undertaking to incur.

As we have already seen, the true essence of the problem is that

[1] *Original Papers*, p. 261.

marginal costs are greater at the peak than at other times. To put the matter loosely, capital costs are to be allocated exclusively to consumers taking at the peak, and in proportion to the amount each takes at that time. It is not uncommon to find cases where prices are for this reason higher at the peak than in slack times. Thus transport undertakings frequently offer cheap tickets in the middle of the day, the telephone system has its cheap night rates, and there are seasonal fluctuations in shipping freights and in hotel charges. Such price differentiation is not price discrimination, or charging what the traffic will bear, for those terms in their proper meaning relate to differentiation based on differences in elasticity of demand, while the differentiation here is due to differences in marginal cost, and is just as likely, if not more so in perfectly competitive conditions as in cases of monopoly.

Nevertheless, while we may say that the "normal" way to allocate standing charges where there are peaks is simply to charge different prices at the peak and in slack periods, it is theoretically possible to achieve the same result with a two-part tariff. If the fixed charge is based not on individual maximum demand but on individual consumption at the time of the station peak, the total charge to any consumer will be the same as it would be if he were charged different prices at different times for a consumption with the same time pattern. This method of allocating standing charges need not be confined to electricity. The season tickets offered by transport undertakings are of the same kind; the holder is expected to travel to and from work at the peak, and makes his contribution to expenses in a lump sum; he is then allowed to travel free at all other times, since the cost of carrying the marginal traveller at other times is negligible. Even the long fluctuations associated with the business cycle could be dealt with in this way, the consumer paying at the beginning of say every ten years a fixed sum based on his consumption during the boom.

In the early days of electricity it was not possible cheaply to record individual consumption according to the time of day, and therefore peak and off-peak consumption could not be charged separately. In these circumstances some early concerns were content to make a charge which did not vary with the hour; but this was clearly inappropriate not only because it allocated part of the standing charges to units consumed in slack periods, but also because the result of so doing was to discourage consumption in the off-peak period when costs are low. The adoption of the two-part tariff in these circumstances was a definite advance on previous practice.

But, if the two-part tariff is to work satisfactorily, the fixed charge paid by each individual really must bear a fairly close relation to the costs that he imposes on the undertaking at the time of the peak. In the early days when peak consumption was confined to lighting demand, the indices on which the fixed charge is usually based—rateable value of the consumer's house, size of the house, capacity of meters, maximum demand—were fairly acceptable guides to the costs imposed by different individuals. But in these days this is no longer the case. The peak is no longer associated with lighting, as far as domestic consumption is concerned; it is associated rather with the use of electricity for heating, whether space heating, water heating, or cooking, and the costs imposed by a consumer who uses electricity for these purposes are several times as great as those imposed by a consumer who uses electricity only for lighting. Size of house and rateable value are useful indices only when all houses use electricity for the same purposes; but in a period, such as the present, when different houses make very different demands, they are most misleading indices for a fixed charge. Even individual maximum demand is now a better guide than size of house, because the persons with high maximum demands are almost certainly using electricity for heating, and almost certainly all coming on to the peak.

The best theoretical solution is still to charge different prices for peak and off-peak consumption. Failing this, the next best would be a two-part tariff with the fixed charge based on appliances in use, so that persons using electricity for heating could be made to bear their full cost, as compared with persons using it only for lighting. A two-part tariff with the fixed charge arbitrarily determined, as at present (e.g. based on rateable value), is both uneconomic, because it overstimulates the peak demand, and unfair because persons who impose high costs on the undertaking pay no more than those who impose low costs. It would be better to have no fixed charge, and to base payments solely on consumption than to have an arbitrary two-part tariff, because consumption is at least a better guide to cost imposed than is rateable value.

We may therefore conclude that as a method of cost allocation where there are peaks in demand and supply, the two-part tariff, suitably framed, is superior to having a single undifferentiated price which discourages off-peak consumption, but inferior to charging different prices at different times, though it may sometimes be more convenient than the latter if the measurement and timing of consumption are costly. This may have been the case when electricity was first being developed, but does not seem to be so any longer. According to Bolton:

"If one were starting *de novo* it would be an easy matter to invent a much more scientific tariff on the costs side, and moreover a perfectly practical one.[1] Undertakings usually know when their peaks will occur, both locally and on the bulk supply. Tariffs would be framed to avoid these times, and for domestic loads they might be, say, 4d. a unit from 4 to 6 p.m. and ½d. all other times. A combined single-phase meter and synchronous clock could be mass produced for about 30s. to 35s., and for another 5s. the makers could probably extend the hands and put it in a bakelite case. It could then hang in the hall and show the time of day (and, incidentally, the rate of charge). An alternative method of changing the timing could be by 'ripple control,' referred to at the end of Chapter VII.

"Such a tariff would require no alternatives and would save all individual assessments and charges whatsoever. It is perfectly easy to understand, particularly after all the publicity recently given to the 'shilling trunk calls' based on exactly the same principle. It represents real costs and at the same time it gives endless scope for heating, cooking, etc., at competitive figures for all times outside the narrow high price zone. However, such ideals (if ideal they are) must be reserved for some brave new world, since the timid old one has chosen other methods and is too fearful of change to be likely to give them up."[2]

III

THE RISK ELEMENT

To conclude that two-part charging, using any of the usual bases for calculating the fixed charge, is an inferior method of

[1] The author adds the cryptic footnote: "I.e. it would work, and in fact has worked. But this is not to say that it would be more satisfactory, in practice, than our present schemes. Experience in Paris suggests that it might not, and anyhow it is far too large a question to be discussed in a sentence."

[2] *Op. cit.*, pp. 208–9.

cost allocation, is not, however, to conclude that it is either an undesirable or an unprofitable method of recovering the standing charges. It may be a method by which a firm protects itself against the risks of unforeseen change.

Let us suppose that an entrepreneur is deciding to invest capital in the form of durable equipment in a certain industry. In doing this he runs the risk that his expectations of the future may be frustrated; if there are new products, new rivals, new inventions, or other unfavourable changes, he may be unable fully to recover the money he is investing. How is he to protect himself against the risk of such changes? From his point of view, the most satisfactory arrangement might be to avoid all risk by getting each potential consumer to pay in advance some proportion of the sum invested. If in the aggregate consumers contributed sums sufficient to cover the capital invested, the entrepreneur would be relieved of all risk of loss. Nevertheless, much as this arrangement might please the entrepreneur, it would be unlikely to please the consumer, who is reluctant to pay in advance for services which he may never use. If this method proved impracticable, the entrepreneur might try as his next best course to get each user to contract to take a minimum quantity of the product, or if payment is by monthly subscription, to subscribe for a minimum number of months—this is a common feature of telephone, gas, electricity and other undertakings. Failing this, the entrepreneur may try to protect himself by securing exclusive contracts, the customer promising not to use the services of any rival undertaking. The list of concerns using such contracts is large; it includes the railway companies, who offer special "agreed charges" to clients who send all their traffic by rail, liner conferences who offer a "deferred rebate," brewers, film distributors, iron and steel concerns, a manufacturer of shoe machinery, and others. Or he may simply offer quantity discounts. All these are methods of tying the consumer to the undertaking, relieving the entrepreneur of the risk of loss due to miscalculations or to changes in demand or supply conditions.

Such devices run counter to the spirit of private enterprise. The essence of that system is that entrepreneurs are the specialists in risk-bearing. It is therefore very difficult to introduce such devices into an industry where entry is unrestricted and easy. There is usually some entrepreneur who is willing to charge the consumer per unit consumed, and to assume himself the risk that over a number of years demand will be large enough for him to recoup all his costs[1]; and where there are such entrepreneurs, consumers are unwilling to be tied by payment in advance or by any exclusive contract. Competitive private enterprise demands that overhead costs shall be recouped not through any fixed charge, as the theory of the two-part tariff suggests, but by inclusion in the variable charge.[2]

The monopolist, too, may meet his overhead costs simply by having a sufficiently high variable charge. But he may choose between doing so and making a fixed charge. He may have a fixed and no variable charge, or a variable and no fixed charge, or some combination of both. The risk of unforeseen change is a strong argument in favour of a fixed charge, which will throw upon the consumer any loss resulting from unfavourable change. Hence unless the entrepreneur is willing himself to bear this risk —and with it the possibility that there may be *favourable* changes —he may seek to impose such a charge. His incentive to insure himself in this way will be particularly great if his product has to face strong competition from other products. For the imposition of a fixed charge in a sense ties the customer to the undertaking, making it worth his while to buy as much as possible from that concern, rather than to divide his purchases, so that his average price may fall as low as possible.

However, the power of the entrepreneur to secure himself in

---

[1] Sometimes it is suggested that in very risky industries no entrepreneur will come forward unless protected either by a monopoly or by special contracts. For instance, the patent system receives some support on the ground that entrepreneurs would be unwilling to try out new inventions unless protected by a monopoly. Similarly combinations in liner shipping are said to be necessary since shipowners would be unwilling to send their ships on regular voyages unless protected against intermittent competition. There seems to be little ground for this view. In the liner case the combinations emerged because there were too many regular sailings, not because there were too few, and their effect was to reduce, not to increase the number. But this is too large an issue to be developed here.

[2] Sometimes part of the "overheads" can be traced to some particular consumer. For instance, a firm may generate its own electricity, but may also connect itself to the public service as an insurance against breakdowns. Where the public station has to instal extra plant as a reserve against this contingency it will make a fixed charge to the firm whether it takes any electricity or not. But in these cases the "overhead" is not an overhead at all; it is a cost directly attributable to the particular consumer, and would not be incurred but for the undertaking to serve him; it is a "customer" cost, as defined in section IV of this paper.

this way depends on the attitude of consumers and on the strength of his monopoly position. It may well be that if a fixed payment is demanded some consumers who are not certain how large their consumption will be will refrain from buying at all. Thus a recent survey of gas undertakings in Great Britain which offer consumers the alternatives of a two-part tariff and a single variable charge shows that a large percentage of those who would benefit by switching over to the two-part tariff fail to do so. Ignorance of the advantages of the two-part tariff may account for this to some extent, but it is also probable that some consumers prefer to remain on the ordinary tariff because they are uncertain how large their consumption is likely to be, and unwilling to commit themselves to the payment of a fixed charge.[1] Where this is an important element, there must be no fixed charge or only a low one, or alternatively consumers must be permitted to choose between a two-part tariff and an ordinary one. Note however that in some cases the element of risk may work the other way. A potential customer may say, "I am unwilling to take this commodity on the basis of so much per unit because I am uncertain how much my family and I will take from time to time, and I may find at the end of the year that we have run up a tremendous bill; I would prefer you to quote me one lump sum charge, and then let us take as much as we like." If the commodity is a new one, or subject to large and unpredictable variations in demand (e.g. one's demand for medical services) the risk element may well favour the imposition of a high fixed charge with a very low or no variable.

IV

THE CONSUMER'S SURPLUS

Another incentive to having a fixed charge is that this may make it possible for the firm to extract some of the "consumer's surplus." The extent to which this is possible depends on the income elasticity of demand for the commodity. If income elasticity is zero, then when a fixed charge is imposed, so long as it is not so high that the consumer ceases to buy altogether, he will buy the same amount at any given marginal price as he would have bought if there were no fixed charge; he will there-

[1] See P. Chantler, *The British Gas Industry*, pp. 127–130.

fore be paying a higher average price for any given quantity than he would be prepared to pay if there were only a variable charge. The effect of the two-part tariff is as it were to shift his demand curve to the right.[1] But this is only so where income elasticity of demand is low. What it boils down to in practice is that the firm will gain from the two-part tariff if customers keep their eyes on the cost of the marginal unit rather than on the total amount spent on the commodity. If the customer watches the size of his bill rather than the marginal price the demand curve facing the firm will be substantially the same whatever system of charging it may use. This point is not always understood. Thus it is some-times suggested that the success of the two-part tariff is proved by the fact that sales expand when a firm adopts it.[2] But this view is fallacious. If the fixed charge is small, the effect of adopting a two-part tariff is to lower the average price at which the com-modity is sold. But if the firm lowered its average price without adopting a two-part tariff sales would similarly expand. The only relevant question is, if the average price had been lowered to the same extent without adopting a two-part tariff, would sales have expanded to the same or a lesser extent? For the two-part tariff is superior only in so far as it enables the firm to sell more at any given average price than it would if average and marginal prices coincided. In some cases this will be so, in others where the customer concentrates on the size of his bill rather than on the marginal price the two-part tariff has not this advantage.

The fact that two different elasticities are relevant when the two-part tariff is used—income elasticity and elasticity of sub-stitution at the margin—is important where two products are highly competitive with each other, as in the case of gas and electricity. The point is not important if one product is a sub-stitute for the other in all uses, for then even if one industry is offering a two-part tariff with a very low variable charge, the consumer will carefully compare his probable total expenditures in using the one product or the other before he commits himself to the payment of the fixed charge. Here competition is deter-mined not just by the marginal price, but also by the amount of

[1] The two-part tariff shares this characteristic with quantity discounts of the "block" type. Wherever the average charge differs from the marginal charge, the demand curve tends to be shifted to the right.

[2] E.g. J. T. Haynes, giving the results of a two-part tariff at Rotherham, makes this claim. *The Two-Part Tariff as an Aid to Gas Sales*, pp. 23–35.

the fixed charge; it is average price that counts.[1] But the position
is different if each product has a use in which it is essential, and
competition is limited to certain additional uses, e.g. if electricity
is considered essential for lighting, and gas for cooking, but they
compete for heating and other purposes. Here since the fixed
charge has to be paid anyway, only the marginal price is relevant.
Each industry may find it profitable so to reduce its variable
charge that it only just covers marginal cost. It is easily shown that
it will not pay to go below marginal cost. Thus in the following
diagram, if DD is the demand curve, OS the marginal cost, and
income elasticity is assumed zero, the maximum consumer's

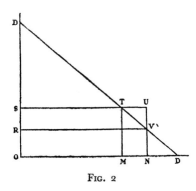

FIG. 2

surplus which can be extracted from this particular consumer by
way of fixed charge is the area DST. If the firm made a variable
charge less than OS, say OR, the consumer would demand ON,
and the firm's net revenue would be a maximum of DST minus
TUV, the fixed charge being increased to DRV. If the variable
charge is to go below marginal cost, it must be for some reason
other than consumer's surplus, such as the reasons already
mentioned. Now marginal cost is not the same as prime cost; it
includes all costs which vary with output. In the long run most
costs, including equipment and expenses of management, vary
with output, and this must be remembered in appropriate circumstances. In the limiting case all the firm's costs are marginal
costs, to be recouped through the variable charge, and if it is

[1] If after making the comparison the consumer chooses the product using
the two-part tariff, he will become tied to the firm, which will then profit if
there should be unforeseen change unfavourable to him. But this is a separate
point which we have already discussed in the preceding section of this paper.

subject to strong competition the firm will be unable to tap consumer's surplus by levying a fixed charge. In general a fixed charge can only be levied if the firm is in a strong monopoly position, or if marginal cost is less than average cost and firms take account of this in their oligopolistic competition with each other.

V

PRICE DISCRIMINATION

Next we come to two-part charging as a form of price discrimination. The effect of making the same fixed charge to all consumers is to discriminate against the small ones. This will pay only if their demands are on the average less elastic than those of large consumers. This is not usually the case, but may be found in special conditions. Thus the small consumer of electricity may be small because he is using it only for lighting, while the large may be using it for heating, power, or other purposes for which the demand is much more elastic than for lighting. One way of meeting this situation would be not to use a two-part tariff, but to charge different prices for current used for different purposes. The two-part tariff, however, serves the same purpose; it is an alternative to rate classification.

Nevertheless it is unlikely that the ability to bear a fixed charge will be the same among all consumers. To avoid discriminating heavily against small consumers, undertakings sometimes have a different fixed charge for each consumer, varying according to the rateable value of his house, the number of rooms, or some similar index. This has indeed the advantage that the fixed charge can be made to increase so rapidly that in effect larger consumers are made to pay higher average prices per unit than smaller consumers, if the smaller are thought to have the more elastic demands.

To avoid frightening off the smaller consumers it is also customary to offer as an alternative to the two-part tariff a single variable charge, somewhat higher than the variable charge of the two-part tariff; the latter is then used only by larger consumers. Or the firm may offer not a two-part tariff but a "block" quantity discount; e.g. it may say, "for the first 20 units, 6d. per unit; additional units at 1d. per unit." This is not so hard on the small consumer, while for the consumer of more than 20 units it has the same effect as a two-part tariff in that the average price differs from the marginal. Here too the size of the first block may vary from consumer to consumer.[1]

Finally, the whole of this discussion so far has been based on the tacit assumption that price discrimination is practicable. This is, of course, only the case if the commodity cannot easily be transferred from those who pay a low price to those who pay a high price. Suppose, for example, that a department store tried to recoup its overhead costs by using a two-part tariff: it might, for instance, offer a 10 per cent discount to any customer who pays a "quarterly subscription" of £2. It would be unlikely to continue the scheme long, because it would soon find that some people were getting goods through subscribing members without themselves paying a subscription. Unless buyers can be isolated from each other, the two-part tariff is an unprofitable method of pricing.[2]

There is, however, one exception to this rule. If a firm is selling to middlemen, a two-part tariff will enable the large middleman to produce more cheaply than the small, if the fixed charge is the same to both, and perhaps to capture his business. The firm may prefer to have only a few large customers, for it may wish them

[1] It has sometimes been suggested that when a firm first introduces the block quantity discount each consumer should have as his first block an amount equal to his previous consumption. But this is not an easy policy to put into effect. J. T. Haynes, who contemplated introducing it in one undertaking he controlled, explains why it was rejected: "It was then proposed that every consumer should be charged a greatly reduced price for all gas used in excess of his normal consumption. This sounded attractive, but examination revealed a number of difficulties. What was a consumer's normal consumption? A large number of typical meter cards were examined, and adjacent houses were found to have widely different consumptions, affected by the number in the family, periods of sickness, inclination or disinclination to use gas, etc. The application of the proposal in such cases would quickly create a sense of unequal treatment between neighbours, and could not be defended by the undertaking in the light of the equal conditions clauses in the Corporation's Gas Acts." See *The Two-Part Tariff as an Aid to Gas Sales*, p. 13. C. L. Paine's proposal (see his article "Some Economic Consequences of Discrimination by Public Utilities," *Economica*, 1937) would be even more difficult to apply than this, because it involves raising the upper price above the level of the previous price and estimating how much each consumer would have bought if this were the only price.

[2] The department store might meet this difficulty by putting a limit on the amount bought on any one subscription, say £30. But then "membership" ceases to correspond to the true two-part tariff, and becomes a means of charging a special price to those who purchase between £20 and £30.

to be able to form a combine to increase their own charges to the public, so that it in turn may be able to share part of their monopoly gains. Trade unionists sometimes for a similar reason urge their employers to combine. In such circumstances the firm will discriminate heavily against small customers, having a fixed charge which is very high relatively to the variable, or even dispensing entirely with the variable and allowing any customer who pays the fixed charge to take as many units as he likes. On the other hand, it is equally likely that the firm may fear that a reduction in the number of its customers might be harmful, since they may be able to combine to force down its charges. In this case it will pursue the opposite policy, discriminating not against the small middleman but against the large. Or again it may particularly want to discriminate against large purchases if the commodity is trade marked and perishable, and it wishes to maintain a reputation for freshness; or to discriminate against small purchases if it wishes to create a reputation of exclusiveness for its products (e.g. cosmetics). Any argument for reducing the number of one's retail outlets is an argument supporting the use of a two-part tariff; any argument in favour of increasing their number is an argument against having a fixed charge.

VI

CUSTOMER COSTS

We have left to the last the case for two-part charging based on the existence of "customer" costs, because, though it seems the most obvious case, to analyse it is to get a summary of the whole problem. "Customer" costs are those costs which have to be incurred if any given customer is to be served, but which do not vary directly with his consumption; such costs as equipping his house with electric wires and fittings, installing a meter and reading it periodically, keeping his account and so on; costs which vary with the number of customers rather than with output.

Suppose, for example, that an electricity concern is supplying electric current, and undertakes to wire premises and instal all necessary fittings. The cost of the installation is an indivisible item which does not vary directly with the amount of current consumed. At first sight it seems quite reasonable to make a separate charge for this, or to use a two-part tariff, basing the fixed charge on the cost of installation, or at least to offer quantity discounts for current. But this is not necessarily the most profitable policy. In suitable circumstances the firm may prefer to make only a fixed charge, supplying the consumer with as much current as he likes without any additional charge. Or on the other hand it may prefer to instal "free of charge," recouping itself for the cost of installation by having a high variable charge. Its fixed charge may be high, low, zero, or even negative (that is to say, instead of asking the consumer to pay for installation, the firm may actually pay him a "rent" for the privilege of installing its equipment on his premises). Similarly, its variable charge may be high or negative; the firm may not merely supply current free, but it may also undertake to repair the equipment free of charge (this being the equivalent of a variable negative) or pay a refund to the consumer if his consumption is large.

This problem is not confined to public utilities; it appears wherever there are complementary goods like gramophones and gramophone records, razors and razor blades, motor cars and tyres, telephone instruments and a telephone service, or other twin commodities one of which is a durable instrument which must be installed before the other can be used. If conditions were suitable a company might give away gramophones to stimulate the sale of records, or give away records to stimulate the sale of gramophones. This poses the question, what is a commodity? In the former case the company would say that it was selling records, the gramophone being only part of the cost of production; in the latter it would be the record that was part of the cost of selling gramophones. The enjoyment of any satisfaction involves a number of separate costs, some of which are indivisible, and it is a problem to decide how many of these indivisible costs are to be treated as different commodities and charged separately, and how many to be merged into a single variable charge. Nor is the problem confined to cases where all costs are undertaken by the same firm. Even if the gramophone companies are separate from the record companies, it may pay one set of companies to subsidise the other; so also it might pay motor car manufacturers to subsidise the sale of petrol, and so on. Given the complementarity it is always the same problem: how high should the fixed charge be relatively to the variable?

We can also fit into the same category another problem which is really only a limiting case of the first. This is the case where the only cost is an indivisible customer cost. An example of this is a case where a firm leases machinery to manufacturers. There is only an installation cost, the cost of the machine. Yet the firm may charge either a fixed monthly rent, or a monthly rent plus a royalty varying with the output of the machine, or a royalty alone with no fixed rental.[1] Wherever a firm is leasing some durable commodity, the use of which is measurable, it can adopt, if it wishes, a two-part tariff as its charge. How high should the fixed charge be?

In competitive conditions the solution is simple: the fixed charge is no more and no less than the cost of installation. But in an imperfect market this is not necessarily the most profitable policy; then all the arguments for and against a fixed charge which we have discussed in the previous sections are once more relevant. The difference now is that we must take as our base for the fixed charge the amount of the installation cost. Arguments in favour of a fixed charge are to be interpreted as supporting a fixed charge greater than the amount of the installation cost; arguments against a fixed charge are arguments for reducing the fixed charge below installation cost, even to zero or a negative price.

Thus the element of risk may serve to reduce the fixed charge below installation cost: consumers may hesitate to wire their premises because they are not sure that their consumption of electricity will justify the initial sum involved, so the firm may assume that risk for them. Or on the other hand it may be the variable charge which they fear, and so the firm may quote a single fixed charge, allowing them to consume as much as they please. Similarly, if potential purchasers of motor cars are deterred by the high initial cost involved, the gasolene companies might profitably subsidise the motor manufacturers, and raise the price of petrol; but if it is the running cost which deters the purchaser, it will be the motor manufacturer who will profitably subsidise the gasolene company, the tyre company, the repair companies, and so on.

The relevance of the two elasticities is as great here as to the allocation of overhead costs. Sometimes by reducing the variable charge one can increase the amount of consumer's surplus to be obtained through the installation charge. At other times, free installation is justified, because it leads to such a terrific increase

[1] A well-known case is that of the United Shoe Machinery Company, which leases machinery to shoe manufacturers on a two-part basis.

in demand for the subsidiary commodity. Discrimination, too, may justify either a high installation and low variable charge, if for instance demand is less elastic in some uses than in others; or a fixed charge less than installation cost and high variable charge, if the firm is selling to middlemen and particularly wants to have a large number of outlets, for example if it is leasing machinery and fears the consequence of a buyers' monopoly. With customer costs, as with standing charges, there is no simple solution; each case must be weighed on its own merits.

Finally, it must be remembered that it may not be worth while making a variable charge at all if the cost of measuring the amount taken by each consumer is high. In the early days of electricity and of the telephone, before simple recording devices were invented, consumers were for this reason charged a lump sum independent of use. Similarly in some countries it is considered that the cost of installing water meters in each house, and reading them periodically, would not be justified. The argument is most forceful where elasticity of demand is not very high, so that consumption is not much greater if unmeasured than it would be if it were measured and charged for. If elasticity of demand is high, and marginal cost high, the argument loses its force.

VII

WELFARE ASPECTS

It remains to consider two-part charging from the standpoint of the public interest. We have seen that from the point of view of the entrepreneur the two-part tariff may frequently be the most profitable method of charging. Can we say that the public interest requires that the fixed charge should be exactly equal to customer cost and that anything more or less is undesirable?

To answer this we must re-examine the incentives to making a fixed charge greater or less than customer cost. The first was that the tariff may be used as a means of allocating overheads where there are peaks in production due to peaks in demand; we saw that it is an inferior method of doing this, even from the standpoint of the entrepreneur, but there is no substantial reason why it should not be adopted if it prove the most convenient. Secondly, a two-part tariff may be a means by which either the entrepreneur or the consumer relieves himself of risk. There is nothing in this inherently contrary to the public interest; but there is some danger of abuse if the consumer is "tied" to one undertaking in competition with others. Especially is this so if the variable charge is reduced below marginal cost, for competition between undertakings must be based on marginal cost if there is to be an "ideal" allocation of resources.

When we come to the two-part tariff as a means of stimulating consumption at the margin the matter is not so simple. It is now generally agreed that the "ideal" output of a concern is such that every consumer is getting every unit for which he is prepared to pay marginal cost.[1] If marginal cost is equal to or greater than average cost, there is no case for a fixed charge; a variable charge equal to marginal cost will cover the total costs of the firm. But if marginal cost is less than average cost, a variable charge equal to marginal cost will not cover total costs. If total costs are to be covered, either the variable charge must be greater than marginal cost, or a fixed charge levied in addition to the variable. It is easily shown that it is better to recoup the difference between average and marginal cost by a fixed charge than to add it to the variable. Consider the following diagram where AD is the demand curve (for convenience a straight line) of a consumer whose income elasticity is assumed to be zero, and ON the marginal cost on the assumption that the cost of supplying this consumer is constant and there is no customer cost. Suppose that the firm was formerly charging a single price OP (average cost), and that it now adopts a two-part tariff with a variable charge ON. This consumer's purchases will then increase from OM to OS, income elasticity being assumed zero. If the amount of the fixed charge is equal to the area PQRN, the consumer will be better off than he was under the previous system since QRT will be added to his consumer's surplus. He will in fact be better off than before so long as the fixed charge is less than PQRN + QRT. This means that two-part charging can benefit both the buyer and the seller better than having a single variable charge, equal to average cost. The danger is that the firm may try to take the whole of the consumer's surplus, ANT, in which case two-part charging becomes the most perfect form of discrimination, and capable of the gravest exploitation. But provided that this danger is guarded

---

[1] There are difficulties in applying this principle to the use of a two-part tariff by public utilities because marginal cost to the undertaking is not necessarily equal to marginal social cost; on this problem see C. L. Paine, *loc. cit.*, pp. 428–431.

against, two-part charging is clearly better than having only a variable equal to average cost, in cases where marginal cost is less than average cost.

Next, an objection raised against two-part charging is that small consumers may have to go without the commodity because they cannot afford to pay the fixed charge. In so far as the fixed charge is being levied as a contribution to overhead costs, this is easily met by an appropriate adjustment of the fixed charge; it is not in the interest of the undertaking, any more than of the public, that the charge should be so high as to exclude anybody. But where the fixed charge is levied to cover customer costs, the

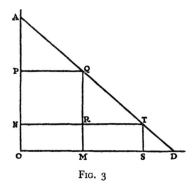

FIG. 3

objection is equivalent to suggesting that some consumers should get the commodity for less than it costs. Thus, in 1933 the Parliamentary Secretary to the Board of Trade explained to representatives of the gas industry why he would oppose any clause permitting a two-part tariff in a forthcoming Bill:

> "I am not attempting to justify the exclusion of the minimum charge from the Bill on any ground of logic or technicality. I am doing it entirely on the political argument that the Government are not prepared to face the opposition that would necessarily come from people in scattered places amounting to millions in total who would never understand the reasons behind a clause of this kind."[1]

An argument like this for compelling the gas industry to supply gas below cost to some consumers and to recover the loss from

[1] *Joint Committee of the House of Lords and House of Commons on Gas Prices* (H.L. 24, 91, H.C. 110), 1937, para. 16.

others does not seem to be strictly within the province of the economist.

Again, two-part charging may be used as a means of increasing or reducing the number of one's retail outlets. For example, it is sometimes alleged that one consequence of two-part charging by the United Shoe Machinery Company has been to maintain an excessive number of small shoe manufacturers. In general we may assume that it is not in the public interest to have a larger or smaller number of outlets than would emerge in conditions of perfect competition. But there is seldom perfect competition either in manufacturing industry or in retail trade. Hence the most that we can say is that the usefulness of two-part charging depends on whether or not it tends to bring about the results which would emerge under perfect competition. For example, if it is used in order to counteract monopolistic tendencies in the outlets it is in the public interest; if it is used to reduce the number of outlets in order to create an illusion of "exclusiveness," it is harmful.

The public's principal safeguard against the abuses of tariff making is competition, which makes exploitation impossible. Where there is little competition, the abuse of two-part charging merges itself into the general problem of the control of monopoly. We cannot take up this subject here in all its ramifications. It is sufficient to point out that in the cases where the two-part tariff is most common there is already some machinery of control. In industry the outstanding case of two-part charging, the shoe machinery case, is based on patent rights; and there already exists under the patent legislation provision for the control of abuses which might well be tightened up. Elsewhere two-part charging is most common in public utilities, the price policies of which are usually subject to regulation in one way or another. Two-part charging can be of great benefit to the public; all that is needed is control adequate to prevent abuse of the power it confers on those who use it.

CHAPTER III

THE ECONOMICS OF LOYALTY

The desire for loyal patronage is almost universal. Every business man seeks to build up that goodwill which brings the customer back again and again. The quality, design and style of an article; its price; the credit facilities provided; free rest rooms; free delivery; advertising; with these and many other services, real or fictitious, firms try to impress their "personality" upon their customers and secure loyal patronage. What is unusual is not the desire for loyalty, but deliberate discrimination against those who are disloyal; and the purpose of these notes is not to study the economics of goodwill in general, but to examine only those cases where there is some differentiation between the loyal and the disloyal customer, whether in price, or in other conditions of service.

This differentiation does not always meet the eye. If a firm or group of firms announces that it will give a discount to customers who undertake never to buy elsewhere, or in extreme cases will refuse to sell at all without such an undertaking, there can be no mistake. But a firm can secure a similar result without any specific demand for loyalty simply by offering quantity discounts of one shape or another, since these make it cheaper to be loyal than to spread one's purchases over many sellers. The boundary between our field of study and other ways of inducing loyalty lies in this element of price differentiation. Tasteful design, branding, advertisement and other devices help to secure loyal patronage, but do not result in the customer getting a better price from the firm if he is loyal than if he is not.

In the following pages we shall first analyse the incentives to this differentiation; then we shall examine some cases of it; and finally we shall enquire how the public interest is affected.

I

THE EFFECTS OF LOYALTY

There are two reasons why a firm may differentiate between loyal and disloyal customers. One is that the costs of supply may be different; the other, that it may be seeking to maintain or extend a monopoly position. Take cost first. Loyalty affects it in two ways, through the economies of quantity buying, and through the economies of regularity.

As for quantity, the loyalty of a customer may reduce costs because his purchases from any one establishment are larger than they would be if he split his custom. It may be cheaper to sell to a customer who comes again and again than to sell the same quantity during the same period to a number of different customers. If the business is done on credit, only one account needs to be kept, and the cost of preliminary enquiries as to credit status is less for one than for many customers (the risk of bad debts, however, may be affected one way or the other). The customer may, on his first visit, examine all the alternative products on sale, and subsequent sales may involve much less sales effort than if the whole range had to be shown to a new customer on each occasion. In brief, there are indivisible elements in selling. Hence customers who come again and again are cheaper to serve than casual customers. There are, of course, disadvantages as well. The loyal customer may waste one's time in gossip; he may consider himself entitled to special treatment, and so on. But in many cases there will on balance be a gain. The analysis of this case is complicated because we more frequently associate the economies of quantity buying with the customer who buys a large amount at a single purchase, and recognise that such a customer may give rise to greater economies, even though disloyal on other occasions, than will a loyal customer buying in driblets. The true comparison is not between large and small purchases, but between sales of a given size to a constant clientele, and sales of the same size to an ever-changing clientele.

The other saving in cost is a function of regularity. If a seller can count on the loyalty of his customers, he can plan his investment more accurately. He also shifts to others losses associated with the risk of fluctuations in demand. In a market where prices are perfectly flexible, and any seller can always dispose of the whole of his output at the market price, there is no incentive to give any special price to loyal customers. One may enter into a contract now to supply some client for the next two years at a price which is below the current market price, but will only do so if one expects months in which it will be compensatingly above the prices then ruling; the quoted price is not a loyalty price, but simply the average of current and future prices. It is in markets with a price floor that it is important to have affiliations. When prices are low, but not low enough to clear the market, that seller is fortunate who has loyal customers. When prices are high, but supplies still less than demand, it pays him, remembering the lean days that lie ahead, to reserve his supplies for those who will support him during the slump, and even to charge such persons a price below the current price.

These two elements in cost, quantity and regularity, provide an incentive to loyalty discounts wholly unconnected with monopoly power, and may emerge even in highly competitive industries. The other incentive to loyalty discounts is that they may in imperfect markets be a device for maintaining or extending monopoly power. Loyalty and innocence are twin virtues. If one is lucky enough to have customers who are prone to either virtue, one may be able to exploit them.

When a seller attempts in an imperfect market to impose exclusive patronage on a customer without offering a sufficiently attractive inducement, the issue resolves itself into a test of strength. If a seller without strong monopoly tries to impose a stipulation of loyalty without the appropriate discounts, his customers will simply leave him to buy elsewhere. He cannot use such a stipulation to *create* monopoly; he can only enforce the stipulation if he already possesses some legal or natural monopoly which compels customers to give him at least some of their patronage, and therefore enables him to penalise them if they withhold the rest. Such monopoly power may be based on a legal privilege such as a patent, copyright, a trade mark, or a licensing system, on ownership of nearly all the sources of some factor of production such as a mineral, or on membership of a combine, and we shall examine some cases in a later section.

Not always does it pay to use monopoly power to compel loyalty. Take the case where a firm has a monopoly for one of its products, but not for the others. It produces X, which is patented, and Y which is unpatented and sold by many competitors. If the purchasers of X also need some Y, it may be tempted to refuse them X unless they also buy all their Y from itself. This will be very profitable if the demand for X is so strong that it will not be much affected by the stipulation; it will not pay if X, though patented, has close substitutes. This is what the Americans call full-line forcing. In its extreme form X and Y will only be sold together. For instance, suppose that a manufacturer of motor cars secures a patent on a carburettor which reduces fuel consumption by 50 per cent. He may decide to reserve such carburettors exclusively to his own make of car, thus using the patent to push his own make; or he may allow rival manufacturers to use the carburettor on payment of a royalty. This extreme type of full-line forcing will only pay if sales of his own car expand so much as to compensate for the royalties which might have been obtained if other manufacturers were allowed the use of the carburettor.[1]

Given the necessary monopoly power, to stipulate that one's commercial customers buy exclusively one's own products may be an alternative to vertical integration. To compel a distributor to stock only one brand is, from the manufacturer's point of view, just one step short of setting up his own retail shops. It is a much safer step. The risks and costs of vertical integration are too well known to require elaboration here. Though there are cases in which it pays, it results generally in loss of the advantages of specialisation. The manufacturer ceases to be a specialist in production, and has to acquire also the techniques of wholesaling and retailing. He has not the same knowledge of local supply and demand conditions as experts in those branches of distribution. His organisation grows so large that it tends to lose flexibility. His distribution costs may be higher than would be those of

[1] The issue sometimes presents itself to the seller in the form, "What is my product unit? Am I prepared to quote separately for every distinct operation or separable component?" For instance, a furniture firm has to decide whether it will sell only suites, or whether individual tables and chairs can be separately bought; and if it decides to sell them separately, whether to sell suites at a price which represents a discount on the aggregate price of component items. Similarly a gramophone company has to decide whether to sell the individual records of a symphony, or to sell them only in sets. In practice the component items can usually be bought separately, a discount being not infrequently offered. There are also cases where they are not sold separately. His Master's Voice sells the Schnabel recording of Beethoven's Waldstein sonata only in sets, and moreover will sell it only to customers who at the same time take the Opus 26. The company explains this by saying that the two sonatas together make up one "volume" out of the fifteen "volumes" issued by its "Beethoven society." But the terminology does not alter the fact that this is an ordinary case of full-line forcing. Putting all the records together may give them extra value for a few people. But there must be many who want the Schnabel Waldstein but not the Opus 26. Full-line forcing pays only if they want the Schnabel Waldstein so badly that they will take the Opus 26 as well, rather than buy some other artist's recording.

independent distributors, pooling his goods with those of many other manufacturers. His range of products is usually more limited than the range stocked by the retailer; if he integrates he may have to buy complementary (even competitive) products from other manufacturers to sell with his own, and the greater the number of such products, the more his business will assume the characteristics of wholesaling and retailing, and the less will he be a specialist in production. These disadvantages of integration are avoided by exclusive dealing arrangements. The retailer is then tied to the manufacturer, but the manufacturer is not tied to the retailer. The advantages of specialisation are preserved, but the manufacturer shifts some of his risks on to the retailer. This he can do only if he has monopoly power. In its absence the retailer will not pledge loyalty unless he is given adequate compensation. Loyalty stipulations cannot be used to create a monopoly; they can only extend or maintain existing privileges.

II

QUANTITY DISCOUNTS

So much for the incentives to differentiation between loyal and disloyal customers. We come now to examine some cases of such differentiation which were found in Great Britain before the outbreak of war. In this section we shall deal with cases where there is no stipulation of loyalty, but the discounts are such that it pays to be loyal; the next will be devoted to cases where loyalty is a specific condition for earning the discount.

All the devices belonging to this section are variations on the theme of the quantity discount—the season ticket, the return ticket, the two-part tariff, coupon trading, all promote loyalty because the price diminishes with quantity bought.

The effectiveness of a quantity discount in promoting exclusive patronage depends in the first place on whether it is "cumulative" or "non-cumulative."[1] A discount is cumulative if the quantity to which it applies is the aggregate quantity purchased during a given period, without reference to the size of the individual purchase. It is non-cumulative if it applies only to the amount taken at a single purchase. Obviously cumulative discounts

---

[1] The terminology is from that very useful and not sufficiently well-known article by W. H. Stevens, "Some Laws of Quantity Discounts," *Chicago Journal of Business*, 1929–30.

promote exclusive patronage to a greater extent than non-cumulative, as the latter are effective only when the article is not expensive to store; then it will pay the purchaser to buy a whole season's stocks from a single seller at one purchase.

The effectiveness of the discount depends also on the rapidity with which the average price falls as the quantity bought increases. There is a difference between discounts where the average price falls in jerks, and those where it falls steadily. The price will fall steadily if the discount given when purchases reach a certain size applies only to additional units taken beyond that point; it will fall in jerks if it applies to the original amount as well. If the price falls in jerks, the exclusiveness of the discounts depends on how close the jerks are to each other. Consider for instance the following terms:—

2 per cent discount on purchases between £5 and £12
3 per cent discount on purchases over £12

If all sellers are offering these terms, a person who habitually buys £11 of the commodity gets the same discount whether he buys exclusively from one seller or buys £5 from one, and £6 from another. The discount is most effective when the upper limit of a range is less than twice the lower limit, thus:—

2 per cent discount on purchases between £5 and £9
3 per cent discount on purchases between £9 and £17

If the price falls steadily this question does not arise. Another difference is that if the average price falls steadily there is a difference between the average price and the marginal price which will have promotional effects, similar to those of the two-part tariff.

Finally, the effectiveness of a quantity discount in promoting exclusive patronage depends on the range of commodities covered by the discount. If the buyer earns his discount for each commodity separately, his incentive to complete loyalty is not as great as if the discount applied to aggregate purchases of all commodities from the same firm. A quantity discount can thus be used as a substitute for full-line forcing.

The reasons for granting the ordinary quantity discount are not difficult to understand. Some are based on economies in cost, arising whether in production, in selling, or in transport, to minimisation of risk, or to differences in elasticity of demand.

This does not mean that every quantity discount can be justified on economic grounds; some are due just to custom or other arbitrary factors, a point which is well illustrated by a writer whose analysis of the discounts offered in certain trades reveals unaccountably wide variations of practice.[1]

Railway policy provides interesting examples of quantity discounts which cannot always be explained. Take the season ticket. There is an economy in issuing one ticket instead of several. The season ticket holder's extra journeys are mainly in slack periods when trains are half-empty. The traveller bears the risk that he may not be able to travel, wherefore the discount on a yearly season is greater than the discount on a monthly season. Loyalty to the railway is secured at the expense of competing motor traffic. The season ticket class as a whole is perhaps more sensitive to charges than the ordinary ticket holders, whose demand is more inelastic. The rate also tapers in the sense that the charge per mile diminishes with distance. This is because the long distance season is used less frequently than the short distance; because the elasticity of demand of the long distance ticket holder is higher, though against this must be set the fact that motor competition is more effective on the shorter journeys; and because differential costs of operating the train are somewhat lower per mile. These are understandable reasons. Yet the evidence given by the railway companies on this subject suggests much arbitrariness in fixing the exact fare.[2] And the principle of the tapering rate, though applied to seasons, is not applied to other passenger fares. The discount on monthly returns is also somewhat arbitrary. In 1926 Sir Ralph Wedgwood informed the Railway Rates Tribunal that the companies had come to the definite conclusion, based on pre-war experience, that the discount was uneconomic, and that having suspended it during the war, the railways had no intention of restoring it,[3] but in 1933 the reduction was reintroduced, at first only in the summer months, to stimulate

<hr/>

[1] "The Relation between the Quantity Purchased and the Price per Unit," by Edward L. Thorndike, *Harvard Business Review*, Vol. XVII, pp. 209 *et seq.*

[2] See *Proceedings of the Railway Rates Tribunal*, April, 1926, Questions 18,088–93, 18,107–9, 18,112, 22,052, 22,061, 22,066, 22,069–70, 22,090–101. Sir Ralph Wedgwood gave evidence as Chairman of the rates and charges committee appointed jointly by the railway companies to prepare evidence for the Tribunal, which was approving the "standard charges" to come into operation on the "appointed day" under the Railways Act, 1921.

[3] *Ibid.*, Questions 17,182–9, 17,194.

holiday traffic, but later as a permanent measure. Since 1926 motor competition has become more intense, and the discount helps to secure loyalty on the return journey. Yet, in view of the language used in 1926, a discount of $33\frac{1}{3}$ per cent takes some explaining.

In analysing the economic basis of quantity discounts there is one pitfall to be avoided. The economies which justify a discount are economies in differential and not in average costs. Average prime costs may be falling for output as a whole, but this is no justification for discriminating between large and small purchases. The acceptance of a large order may enable a firm to reach a scale at which, for instance, it can buy its raw materials very cheaply, but this is no case for discrimination. If total costs are the same whether a firm handles one large order or many small ones of the same aggregate amount, there is no reason to offer quantity discounts. The fact that you can get a quantity discount on your purchases is no reason for giving a quantity discount on your sales; it is only an argument for quoting to both large and small buyers a price low enough to extend your output to the point where marginal revenue will equal marginal cost. The popular view that a large purchase deserves a special price because it "reduces overheads" has no economic foundation.

At the same time, even where there are real economies in quantity selling, a firm may nevertheless refuse to offer quantity discounts. One reason may be to avoid arguments over repeat orders; where the economy is one which justifies a non-cumulative but not a cumulative discount, repeat orders sometimes cause trouble, as the customer may expect to get as good a price for a small repeat order as he did for the original large order. Another reason may be to avoid restricting one's outlets. The offer of quantity discounts enables large middlemen customers to drive their smaller rivals out of the market, so that the supplier may find himself at the mercy of one, or a few, large customers. Or the reason may be that some customers exert pressure to prevent discounts from being allowed to rival customers who would otherwise qualify for them, as when wholesalers insist on the "classification" of customers, to prevent large retailers from receiving the same "trade" discounts as wholesalers buying similar quantities. This may also work the other way, large retailers insisting on receiving quantity discounts to the disadvantage of small retailers, where there are actually no substantial economies in quantity selling. Or the firm itself may prefer to give such discounts even in the absence of economies, because it wishes to eliminate small customers (middlemen or manufacturers), either so that its large customers may make monopoly gains in which it can share, or because it believes that restricting the number of retailers handling its product to a few "high class" firms will give its product a reputation for exclusiveness on which a monopoly price policy can be based. In the fixing of trade discounts, political strategy is often the major consideration.

Finally, a note on coupon trading. There is no need to repeat the analysis of the reasons why manufacturers use this form of sales promotion, the types of product suitable for coupon trading, its cost, or the organisational factors already discussed in an extensive literature.[1] Suffice it to note that coupons are very efficient promoters of loyal patronage because the seller must continue with the same brand until he has collected a minimum number of coupons, or the number he requires for redemption in "free gifts." The same applies to trading stamps, which do for the retailer what the coupon does for the manufacturer, and, to a lesser extent, to cigarette cards.[2][3]

III

LOYALTY CONDITIONS

Cases in which exclusive patronage is specifically demanded as a condition for special treatment are not by any means as common

[1] The fullest report on the position in Great Britain is the *Report of the Committee on Gift Coupons and Trading Stamps*, Cmd. 4385, 1933; two pamphlets, *The Case for Gift Coupon Advertising*, published by the Advertising Manufacturers and Distributors Association, 1933, and *The Case against Coupon Trading*, Anon., 1933, are also useful, especially the former for its statistics not obtainable elsewhere. Useful American articles are I. M. Rubinow, "Premiums in Retail Trade," *Journal of Political Economy*, 1905, and A. R. Sommer, "Premium Advertising," *Harvard Business Review*, Vol. X.

[2] The history of cigarette cards and organisation of the card market are described in I. O. Evans, *Cigarette Cards*.

[3] The dividend paid by co-operative societies resembles the trading stamp, and is often called a loyalty dividend. It does not fall within our scope, however, because there being no minimum set to purchases, as with trading stamps and coupons, the customer does not pay a higher net price to the shop the less loyal he is. Some societies, but not all, do not pay dividends on non-member purchases. The authoritative study of the subject is J. A. Hough, *Dividend on Co-operative Purchases.*

as the quantity discount device. They are mostly cases where a group of firms is trying to crush competitors who have stayed outside the ring; but there are also cases where individual monopolists have felt strong enough to use the device.

A well known case is the "tied" public-house. The licensing system of Great Britain limits the sale of liquor to licensed premises, and is designed to restrict their number. Consequently the brewer is induced to buy up premises. A House of Commons Committee in 1817 reported that already half the houses in the Metropolis were controlled by brewers.[1] By 1899, according to the Royal Commission on Liquor Licensing Laws, 75 per cent of the houses in the country were so controlled,[2] and by 1931 the figure had risen to 95 per cent.[3] Some of these brewer-owned houses are operated by salaried managers, but the majority are leased to tenants, the tenant being the licensee recognised by the law. And in every case the brewer imposes on his tenant a condition that he shall purchase beer exclusively from the lessor. In many cases he goes even further, compelling the tenant to take not only beer but also his wines, spirits and even matches and sawdust through the brewer, who supplies them usually at a price above the market rate. On the other hand, the rent charged for the house is usually below the market rate, so that it is not easy to compare the position of licensees who own their own houses with that of tied tenants. Whether the brewer can exploit the tenant depends on whether that class of person is restricted in his choice of occupation; that he can use the tie to exploit the public is due to the licensing system preventing the building of competing houses.

Another famous case is that of the United Shoe Machinery Company. This company was formed in the United States in 1899 to buy up existing companies, and by 1910 controlled 90 per cent of the shoe machinery industry in that country. Most of its machinery is not sold, but let out on lease to manufacturers, and in 1901 it introduced a new lease with tying clauses; any manufacturer using any of its most important machines had to pledge himself in effect not to use any machinery made by any other firm, and as the company held patents for some of the best and

[1] *Royal Commission on Liquor Licensing Laws*, 1898, Vol IX, p. 116 (Reprint of Committee's Report). [2] Final Report, p. 96.
[3] *Royal Commission on Licensing (England and Wales)*, 1929–31, Report, para. 295.

most advanced machinery in the industry, it was thus able to compel manufacturers to resort to it exclusively as well for other machines not covered by patents. The company duly extended its activities to the United Kingdom, where, with the help of these leases, it now controls 90 per cent of the trade.[1] Since the Patent Act was revised in 1907, manufacturers must now have the option of free leases, but the rental on these terms is so much higher than the rental on tied terms, that the option is not of much practical value.

A third case is the use of the copyright privilege by American film renters (the wholesalers of the industry) to tie up the outlets. Until the passage of the Cinematograph Films Act in 1927, "block booking" was a common practice; a renter controlling a good film with a popular star would refuse to let an exhibitor have it unless he contracted also for others which he would not otherwise have taken. The large companies controlling chains of theatres could not be exploited in this way, but the one-cinema exhibitor is weak, and renters have kept him so by refusing to recognise exhibitor co-operatives.[2] So firm a hold did the American producers get through this device that Parliament was persuaded in 1927 to prohibit "blind booking" (i.e. the booking of films before they are trade shown), and to restrict advance booking to a period not exceeding six months, thus limiting severely the number of films which can be forced on an exhibitor at any given time. This Act (tightened up in 1937) has reduced the extent of the practice, but it still persists.

Apart from these three cases, all the other important instances of exclusive dealing arrangements are due to pressure by combinations of firms. The pattern is that of the labour market, where many trade unions have long insisted on the closed shop. Trade combinations seem to have started to follow this model after about the 1870's. The best known examples where exclusive terms are, or have once been offered, are the unsuccessful attempts of the

[1] Accounts of the company's activities in the United Kingdom are given in the *Report of the Departmental Committee on the position of the Engineering Trades after the War*, 1917, and the *Report of the Committee on Trusts*, 1919. The company's methods are attacked in *The Growth of a Monopoly*, a pamphlet published in 1918 by the British Boot Machinery Manufacturers' Association, and defended in Richard Roe, "The United Shoe Machinery Company," *Journal of Political Economy*, 1913–14.

[2] On this whole question see *Cinematograph Films Act, 1927, Report of a Committee appointed by the Board of Trade*, Cmd. 5320 of 1936.

Birmingham Alliances,[1] the Scotch Boiler Plate Association,[2] the White Lead Convention,[3] and the cotton spinners[4]; and the more successful attempts of the Bradford Dyers Association,[5] the shipping conferences,[6] the National Light Castings Association,[7] the Tin Plate Conference,[8] various other groups in the iron and steel industry,[9] the Greystone Mortar Association,[10] the Midland Pipe Association,[11] the Electric Cable Makers' Association,[12] the Electric Lamp Makers' Association,[13] the Wallpaper Manufacturers,[14] and the railway companies.[15] Space forbids an analysis of each of these cases; we select only those which best illustrate the common problems.

Every trade combination, unless protected by special legislation, is subject to internal and external stresses which threaten to wreck it. The external stress is the competition of firms outside the ring; the internal stress the quarrels of members over quotas and prices. The ring is most secure from outside competition if its members own nearly all the sources of some mineral, or if the optimum technical unit is so large that only firms with large financial resources can hope to establish themselves in the industry; or if the group is protected by some legal privilege such as trade marks, patents or tariffs. If by reason of its special privilege the group can count on each of the buyers in the market having to come to it at some time or other, it can impose such heavy penalties for disloyalty that they all pledge themselves to it. But if outside the group are firms able to supply all the requirements of the market, customers are not at the mercy of the group, and there is little reason to think that the mere adoption of exclusive terms will enable a group to establish and retain a monopolistic position.

Thus in the Lancashire cotton industry attempts have been

---

[1] H. W. Macrosty, *The Trust Movement in British Industry*, p. 79.
[2] *Ibid.*, p. 67.   [3] P. Fitzgerald, *Industrial Combination in England*, p. 118.
[4] *Infra.*   [5] Macrosty, p. 155; Fitzgerald, p. 20.
[6] A full account of their origins, failures and successes is in the report and evidence of the *Royal Commission on Shipping Rings*, 1906–9; there is an inferior discussion in the *Report of the Imperial Shipping Committee on the Deferred Rebate System*, 1923.   [7] Fitzgerald, p. 48.
[8] *Ibid.*, p. 44.   [9] D. L. Burn, *History of Steel Making*, p. 342, and *infra*.
[10] Fitzgerald, p. 110.   [11] *Ibid.*, p. 112.
[12] *Ibid.*, p. 122.   [13] *Ibid.*, p. 124.   [14] *Ibid.*, p. 155.
[15] See L. A. Carey, *Modern Railway Practice*, Ch. X, G. Walker, *Road and Rail*, Ch. II, and *infra*.

F

made for some years to fix and maintain prices above the competitive level, groups of firms in each section signing agreements not to sell below a given minimum price. One such agreement, signed in 1937, covered nearly 90 per cent of the firms in the Egyptian mule spinning section, and as the position was being undermined by the outside firms, the signatories tried in November 1938 to strengthen their position by offering a discount of 5 per cent to all customers who undertook to patronise the group exclusively. The manœuvre failed; price net of rebate continued to exceed that of the outsiders, who accordingly lost no customers. The offer was therefore withdrawn in April 1939.

The fate of rebates in the iron and steel industry was similar, though this was their home. They flourished in one or two specialised sections, but not in the major ones. The failure of pre-1914 rebates in steel manufacture has already been described by Burn.[1] In 1926 new associations were started in the steel section which included practically all the British steel manufacturers. The competition they had to face was that of the continental producers. In 1927 this was intensified, and in reply to it a rebate varying from 5s. per ton on steel ship plates to between 5s. and 12s. 6d. per ton (a quantity discount) on joists and angles was granted to all buyers who signed an agreement to use only British steel. By the end of 1927 80 per cent of British steel users had signed. To coerce the remaining 20 per cent prices were advanced 5s. per ton in February 1928, and the loyalty rebates simultaneously increased by 5s.; so that loyal buyers paid the same net prices as before, but others were at a disadvantage of from 10s. to 17s. 6d. on all steel bought at home. "So long as foreign supplies were cheap and plentiful," Messrs. Wm. Jacks & Co. comment,[2] "that did not matter." Buyers who depended mainly on British steel pledged loyalty; the others continued to get the bulk of their supplies from abroad. In 1928 and 1929 continental prices rose, and were above British steel prices, which were kept stable; this drove some buyers to sign the pledge. Then in 1930 and 1931 came the real test. British prices were maintained, but continental prices fell below them. To strengthen its hold, the association increased the rebates in January 1931; there was, nevertheless, much fear that the schemes would break down, and

[1] Loc. cit., p. 342.
[2] *Annual Review of the Iron and Steel Trades in 1928*, p. 18. This account is summarised from the pages of the firm's Annual Reviews, 1927–32.

a clamour for a tariff began which was satisfied in 1932. Without this tariff it is doubtful how much longer the rebates would have been effective. The subsequent history of rebates in the industry is interesting, because they have now been put to a new purpose. The Iron and Steel Federation was formed in 1934, and in 1937 had 27 constituent associations. Its hold over these associations being weak, it decided to use loyalty rebates to strengthen it. Each association is encouraged to give a rebate to such customers as pledge themselves (*a*) to purchase exclusively from firms within the Federation and (*b*) to belong to one of the constituent associations of the Federation. The idea is that if any firm breaks away from its own association, all other associations will come to the rescue by withholding from the offender all rebates on all his raw materials. The signal to do this, however, must come from the Federation, which is thus able to withhold support from associations whose policy it disapproves.[1]

In shipping, the amount of capital required to start a new liner service facilitates monopoly. But even here, and despite the particularly onerous terms of the rebate, the conferences have not had it all their own way. In the days before 1914, when the industry was prosperous, many new companies broke into the conferences. The rebate system is most effective in warding off sporadic competition by tramps, but is unable to prevent all competition. Where the commodity is one for which the tramp is most suitable, or one which can be accumulated and sent by tramp, e.g. coal, rice, sugar, the deferred rebate system cannot be applied to it, and the shipper is free to patronise the tramp without forfeiting rebates on other commodities; he is also always free to charter a whole ship without forfeiting rebates though he is penalised if he sends less than a full cargo by tramp. The rebate system strengthens the hands of the conferences, but does not confer unlimited power on them.

A new case of loyalty provisions is the "agreed charge" which railways are allowed to make under the Road and Rail Traffic Act of 1933. The feature of this charge is generally that if the consignor agrees to send all his traffic by rail he gets a special quotation. It is designed to meet motor competition, and the limits to its success depend on the strength of motor competition. Only a small number of consignors have entered into agreements;

[1] See *Import Duties Advisory Committee, Report on the Iron and Steel Industry*, 1937.

and in a number of cases part of their traffic is pledged, but not all, and allowance also made for the consignor to do his own delivery within a specified local range. Another special feature of these agreements is that the freight is calculated per parcel (ton, etc.) without reference to distance carried. The major incentive to this break with all railway traditions is said to be that it reduces clerical work, since the number of parcels has to be counted, but no account need be taken of classification or distance. This system has its dangers. The price quoted per parcel is less than the usual price for long-distance work and greater than the price of short distance. The consignor has, therefore, an incentive to do the short distance work himself, or get other contractors to do it, but this is frustrated by requiring him to send all his traffic by railway, or at least imposing restrictions on the amount not so sent. He is now also able to compete more effectively in distant markets, so there is a progressive tendency for the average length of haul to increase, and the charge has regularly to be revised. From the social point of view the flat rate is undoubtedly uneconomic, because it causes cross-hauling. Having promoted the charge in 1933, the Ministry of Transport has had to cope since the outbreak of war with some of its anti-social results.

IV

IN THE BUYERS' MARKET

We have written so far as if in all exclusive dealing arrangements it is the seller who is seeking to tie the buyer. This is by no means the case. The buyer in many markets has just as great an incentive to tie the seller. The quantity discount is paralleled in agriculture, where higher prices are usually paid for large quantities than for small parcels of produce. Exclusive arrangements are found in the sale of the goodwill of businesses, the training of apprentices, and the grant of exclusive agencies by manufacturers to distributors—to take only a few of the well-known examples. Buyers' combinations are exemplified in the Report of the Board of Trade Committee on Restraint of Trade, 1931, which described the pressure retail trade associations bring to bear on manufacturers to stop supplies to retailers who are cutting prices or infringing distance or other restrictions. The habits of such associations in the grocery trades, tobacco, stationery, newsagencies, motor agencies, cycle trades, and the photography trade[1] need no further description. We shall illustrate their problems from the history of a new association which has emerged since that committee reported.

The retail prices of proprietary drugs are fixed, and any chemist who undercuts them is penalised by having his supplies stopped through the machinery of the Proprietary Articles Trade Association. This association, which is adequately described elsewhere,[2] protects the chemist against price competition, but not against an increase in numbers, one of the consequences of price maintenance itself. He would like to see the number of chemist shops reduced, whether by imposing a distance limit, as in the newsagent's trade, or by tightening up qualifications. So far nothing has been done to limit the number of chemist shops, but steps have been taken to prevent competition with chemists by other retailers. The object of the "Chemists' Friends Association" is to persuade manufacturers to sell medicinal products exclusively through qualified chemists, and to stop selling through grocers, barbers, cafés and other outlets. Manufacturers who undertake to do this are enrolled in the association, on the council of which they are represented. And to ensure control over all outlets, wholesalers are included in the scheme. Where a manufacturer believes that his retailers should have special qualifications, as in the photographic trade, there is little difficulty in persuading him to join such an association. The "Chemists' Friends" has met its full quota of opposition. To coerce manufacturers, retail chemists refuse window display or other sales promotion to the products of manufacturers who refuse to join. Manufacturers of extensively advertised products are able to withstand this pressure, but the losses in the ensuing struggle are frequently severe. At the end of 1939 over 100 manufacturers had already capitulated, and the fall of other big concerns was confidently predicted.

V

WELFARE ASPECTS

Should these exclusive arrangements be tolerated? Is it antisocial to reward the loyal customer with a special price? The

[1] The Joint Council in this trade has been discontinued since the Committee reported, but its functions continue to be performed by the manufacturers' association.

[2] In the Report, and in E. T. Grether, *Resale Price Maintenance in Great Britain.*

official commissions reporting *ad hoc* on specific cases have adopted no consistent view; in shipping, the iron and steel industry and retail trade exclusive arrangements have been blessed; in the liquor trade, the film industry, and engineering they have been condemned.

The first difficulty in answering these questions is the fact that such arrangements are not always harmful. In so far as loyal patronage secures economies, it should be encouraged, and the loyal patron rewarded. The economies are frequently exaggerated. Those who believe that after the war the housewife should have to continue to register with particular shops point out that if each butcher in the street knows every week to expect fifty customers, stocks carried and waste are smaller than if one week one butcher gets a hundred customers and the other none, and the distribution of customers from week to week is completely unforeseeable. This is true, but not very realistic. And yet in so far as loyal patronage facilitates planning, the loyal should be encouraged. There is no case for compulsory loyalty, but there is a case for a loyalty rebate where the economies are real. In such circumstances the consumer should retain his freedom to choose between loyalty and the right to change his seller for whatever reason seems good to him. If he exercises this right he must pay the full cost, in forfeiting the rebate given to loyal customers. To compel loyalty violates consumers' freedom; provided they are prepared to pay the cost of it, this seems to be a freedom which might well be retained, as anyone who has experienced the discourtesies of shop-keepers will appreciate. Let him who wishes to be loyal get a rebate.

The real point is that such rebates only become harmful in the hands of monopolists in a position to exploit them. Even in the hands of monopolists, we can only condemn the rebate if we condemn the monopoly. The commissioners who supported exclusive arrangements in shipping, iron and steel, and retail trade, did so because they believed that in those trades monopoly is more desirable than competition. Whether they were right or not, the principle is accepted that there are a few industries in which monopoly may lead to economies not realised in competition; there exclusive arrangements are clearly desirable.

It follows that exclusive dealing ought to be prohibited, but only in the hands of monopolists, and that provision should be made for excluding desirable monopolists. In England there has been no specific legislation against it,[1] except for an ineffective provision in the Patent Act, and the courts have rather surprisingly decided that it does not violate the common law prohibition of restraint of trade.[2] In the United States, however, section 3 of the Clayton Act declares that:

It shall be unlawful for any person . . . to lease or make a sale or contract for sale of goods . . . or fix a price charged therefor, or discount from, or rebate upon, such price, on the condition . . . that the lessee or purchaser thereof shall not use or deal in the goods . . . of a competitor or competitors of the lessor or seller, *where the effect of any such lease, sale or contract . . . may be to substantially lessen competition or tend to create a monopoly in any line of commerce.*

The greatest difficulty in enforcing this section has been the words in italics, as it has been left to the courts to determine the line between monopoly and competition. Courts are not competent to do this; the line must be drawn in the Act itself. A monopolist might be defined for legislative purposes as any person who has a patent, copyright, trade mark, brand, licence or other privilege protected by the law; any person whose purchases or sales amount to one-third of the total sales of the commodity in the United Kingdom; or any person acting in combination with other buyers or sellers. Any monopolist who considered it to be in the public interest that competition be suppressed in his industry should have the right to apply to the appropriate minister (say the President of the Board of Trade) for exemption from the provisions of the law, and the Minister, if satisfied that a *prima facie* case existed, should refer it to a commission for public enquiry, and act according to its report; on condition that he must lay down terms regulating the prices, profits and other circumstances of each monopolist to whom he grants exemption.[3]

[1] As a wartime measure the Prices of Goods Act forbids refusal to sell one commodity except on condition that the buyer takes simultaneously some other commodity. This is really an attack on one of the methods of evading price control.   [2] *United Shoe Machinery Co. v. Brunet* (1909), A.C. 330.

[3] Some supervision already exists, but it is inadequate. The Comptroller of Patents has some power to redress abuses; so has the Railway Rates Tribunal; the Import Duties Advisory Committee can bring some pressure to bear on the iron and steel industry; and the Imperial Shipping Committee and the Cinematograph Films Council can give publicity to abuses in their respective industries. More adequate controls need to be established, with fuller powers, but this is not the place to discuss the subject.

In this way desirable monopolies would be supervised, and the undesirable prevented from using loyalty rebates to extend their power. The Clayton Act prohibited only sellers' exclusions; prohibition of buyers' exclusions is also desirable to put an end to trade boycotts.

The other difficulty in enforcing this type of legislation is the fact that there are effective substitutes for loyalty rebates. One is the use of quantity discounts. In America the Robinson-Patman Act has dealt with this, by placing on the person granting such discounts the onus of proving that there really are corresponding economies. Another substitute is to put different commodities together and call them one commodity, thus compelling people who want x to buy y also. In *Federal Trade Commission v. Gratz et al.*,[1] the Supreme Court allowed this evasion; it would have to be forestalled by specific provision in the Act. Yet another substitute is to use a contract of agency instead of a contract of sale[2]; this means that exclusive agencies must be prohibited no less than exclusive sales and leases. The fourth substitute is not so easily dealt with. It is vertical integration. If a manufacturer is prevented from tying his retailers, he will be tempted to set up his own retail shops; vertical integration has been marked in the cinema industry since the restrictions on block booking, though, of course, other and more important factors were also at work in the same direction. To prohibit loyalty rebates without prohibiting vertical integration is to leave a gap.

The fact is that loyalty rebates are only one weapon in the hands of a would-be monopolist. A law prohibiting them is a useful part of an anti-monopoly programme, but it is only a part. There must be simultaneous revision of the patent law, provision of credit facilities for small firms, prohibition of price and quota agreements and associations, and supervision of industries where monopoly is considered desirable, whether through tribunals like the Railway Rates Tribunal, or through operation by public corporations. We cannot end or control monopoly simply by prohibiting loyalty rebates; but if we wish to end monopoly, such legislation should be an integral part of the programme. Here in Britain we continue to laud the virtues of competitive private enterprise almost without realising the extent to which our

[1] 253 U.S. 421 (1920).
[2] *Federal Trade Commission v. Curtis Publishing Company*, 260 U.S. 568, 574 (1923).

economy has ceased to be competitive. This remains almost the only important country without legislation to keep the market free, or at least a general law to control the activities of trusts. If private groups are not to submerge the public interest, Parliament must take bold anti-trust action after the war, and now is the time to prepare its programme.

CHAPTER IV

THE INTER-RELATIONS OF SHIPPING FREIGHTS[1]

Our purpose in this chapter is to examine the connection between the different rates quoted for the use of tramp ships. In the past the literature of shipping has been content to dismiss this subject by saying that all such rates move together in the same direction except inward and outward rates, which move inversely. Our generation, however, requires more precise information. Until 1935 the tramp shipping market was one of the most competitive in the world, and the analysis of its behaviour was of academic rather than practical importance. But when in 1935 a price-fixing committee was established it became important to know the precise relations between different rates, and to examine the effects of fixing some rates while leaving others free. In the first half of this paper we shall analyse the pre-1935 relations, using some of the index numbers which have been published since the end of the last war. The second half of the paper will examine the effects of freight control.

I

VOYAGE AND TIME CHARTERS

Let us begin by examining the relation between voyage charter rates and time charter rates. A voyage charter is a contract of hire for a specific voyage, say from Australia to the United Kingdom; a time charter is a contract of hire for a specific period of time, which may be long enough for several voyages. The time charter rate is therefore normally a "long term" rate, and the voyage charter rate a "short term" rate. Before the war of 1914–18 twelve months was about the "normal" period for a time charter, and two- and three-year charters were not uncommon; but in the

---

[1] This paper owes much to conversations with Mr. W. T. Stephenson and to correspondence with Mr. E. A. V. Angier, Mr. G. H. Hopkins and Dr. L. Isserlis, none of whom, however, is committed to its conclusions. Some of the computations are the work of the Economic Research Division of the London School of Economics.

post-war decades charterers (i.e. the persons who hire from the owners) have been less willing to commit themselves; six months has become the normal, and time charters for so short a period as one voyage are quite common. There are, however, marked cyclical fluctuations in the period of the modal time charter. When conditions are booming, and rates expected to rise, charterers are anxious to cover their tonnage requirements for longish periods, and twelve month charters become quite common. When conditions are expected to decline charterers are less anxious to commit themselves, and periods of less than six months are the rule. Owners, too, are not keen on long time charters when rates are low, as an upward turn during the period may be accompanied by a rise in running costs. There are similar fluctuations in the volume of business, since the liner companies, who charter to meet temporary increases of demand in regular trades, are naturally most active at the height of a boom in world trade.

Time charter rates are linked with voyage charter rates both on the supply side and on the demand side. On the supply side, the shipowner has the alternative of seeking a time or a voyage charter. On the demand side, some merchants are indifferent as between time and voyage charters and even if this were not so, speculators would take ships on time charter and re-let them on voyage charter if the former rate were out of step. The two rates must therefore move together.

By analogy with the capital markets, the current time charter rate should be equal to the average of current voyage futures. To put it broadly, the time charter rate should depend not so much on the current voyage rate as upon the expected trend of voyage rates in future months. If rates (and/or running costs) are expected to rise, it should be above the current voyage rate; if they are expected to fall, it should be below it. Such market reports as we have comparing time charter rates for short periods with time charters for long periods support this conclusion. For example, 1904 was a bad year for shipping: short charters therefore were available at a discount on long charters:

"For the trade with the West Indies, etc., a very large number of steamers have been taken up; those over about 4,000 d.w. for two or four months at rates varying from 2s. 9d. to 3s. on deadweight. . . . For longer periods, say six to twelve months or twelve months, rates were about 3d. to 4½d. more all round."[1]

The first nine months of 1937, on the other hand, saw rising freights; the rates for short and long charters were less than the rates for medium periods:

"For round voyages from about 4s. 9d. to 7s. 3d. was paid. Longer periods were worth, say about four months, 5s. 1½d. to 6s. 9d.; six to nine months 5s. 9d. to 8s.; about twelve months 4s. 9d. to 7s. 6d.; and about eighteen months about 5s. 3d."[2]

Further confirmation is available from another source. The Chamber of Shipping has published an index number of time charter rates month by month from 1920 to 1937.[3] It has also published an index of voyage charter rates in the same period, both indices having 1920 as the base year. In comparing these indices we must remember that the voyage rate reported in any month is not strictly a "spot" rate. During a slump there is usually idle tonnage at or near most ports, and the average voyage charter is for a ship to be available within a very short time. In a boom, on the other hand, ships are booked up in advance; ships ready for immediate loading are not easily available, and if they were their price would be above that of ships not required for another two or three months. The rates actually reported in any month and incorporated in the index are therefore "futures" rates rather than "spot" rates, and are lower than the spot rates would be. This means that in boom years the voyage charter index is somewhat lower than it would be if business were done on spot terms, and this must be remembered in comparing it with the time charter index.[4] The latter is based on the rates for a six months ship.

· [1] E. A. V. Angier, *Fifty Years' Freights*, p. 118. This volume is a collection of the market reports circulated by the Angier Brothers during the years 1869 to 1919. For the student of shipping markets it is a goldmine.

[2] "Angier's Shipping Report for 1937," in *Fairplay* for January 13, 1938. For other examples of the difference between long- and short-period rates see, e.g. *Fifty Years' Freights*, pp. 136, 143; "Angier's Shipping Report for 1926" in *Fairplay* for January 6, 1927.

[3] See *Annual Reports* of the Chamber of Shipping. The indices also appeared monthly in the *Statist*. For details as to their construction, see the *Statist*, October 29, 1921.

[4] In making comparisons still further difficulties arise from the fact that the voyage index is underweighted for outward voyages and for voyages which

Chart I shows these indices on a logarithmic scale. It will be seen that when the indices are equated for 1920 the time charter index lies below the voyage charter index in most years, but rises above it on certain occasions. It is to the margin between them that we must direct our attention.

Let us begin with the last year of the series. Autumn 1936 to Autumn 1937 was a boom year. Charterers rushed to cover their future requirements by booking ships well ahead. The time charter rate therefore rises much more rapidly than the voyage charter rate. In fact an unusual situation developed; as the time charter market is small relatively to the voyage charter market it is usually the latter which dominates. But in 1937 so much business was done in time charters that for some time it was the time charter rate which pulled up the voyage charter rate. In the picturesque phrase of the market, the tail was wagging the dog. Towards the end of the year the boom ended, the time charter index again fell below the voyage charter index.

Running our eye backwards along the chart we come to the last quarter of 1935, when the time charter index is again above the voyage charter index. This was due to the Abyssinian war. At its outbreak the market thought that there might be a general conflagration leading to a greatly increased demand for ships. Charterers extended their operations in the time charter market, and owners, anticipating a good future, demanded higher rates for long periods than for short. Within a month or two, however, it became clear that the Abyssinian affair would not have as great an influence as had been expected; the time charter index sank back to its position below the voyage charter index.

1931–34 were bad years. Owners, however, were always on the look-out for the end of the slump. The time charter index is therefore very sensitive. When the voyage rate shows a tendency to rise owners pick up courage hoping that this at last is the end of the slump; the time charter index shoots up more rapidly than the voyage charter index, and then slumps down again when it becomes clear that the rise was only temporary. This explains the

neither commence nor end in Europe. Despite these defects, however, I believe that the comparisons can still usefully be made. Some of the defects have been remedied in the Chamber's new index number started in 1935. For a discussion of the index number problem see L. Isserlis, "Tramp Shipping, Cargoes and Freights," in the *Journal of the Royal Statistical Society*, 1938.

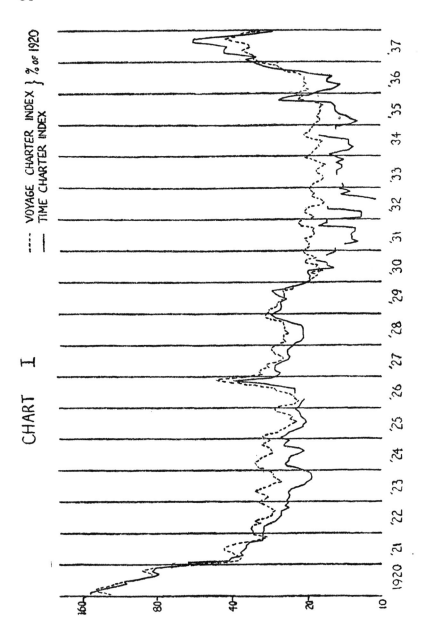

CHART I

last quarter of 1931, the second quarter of 1932, and the third quarter of 1934.[1]

During 1929 and 1930 voyage charter rates were falling. At first owners refused to believe that the fall could be very large or very long; they held up the time charter rate, and the voyage index fell below the time index. Even when it was realised that we were in for a major slump, the time charter index fell slowly and reluctantly. Whereas the voyage charter index reached its low levels early in 1930, the time charter index did not get down to its depression bed until a year later. This phenomenon is exactly paralleled in the 1920 slump. The voyage charter index fell rapidly to the end of 1921, and more slowly thereafter. The time charter index fell slowly until the end of 1921, and then for the next two years much more rapidly than the voyage charter index.

The other period which calls for special mention is the last quarter of 1926. The consequence of the coal strike in the latter half of that year was to stop the export of British coal. There were consequently no outward cargoes to contribute towards the expenses of ships; inward cargoes had to bear the full burden. The Chamber of Shipping's Voyage Charter Index, which is heavily overweighted for inward voyages,[2] shows an increase which is misleading. An index number which took account of the fact that outward cargoes were no longer available would show a much smaller increase. At the same time, there was an increased demand for shipping, and it is not inconceivable that the time charter index would lie above a voyage charter index duly weighted for outward cargoes.

We can now sum up the relation between time and voyage rates as follows. The two markets are connected and rates move together. But time charter rates fluctuate more widely than voyage charter rates. When conditions are improving, long rates rise more rapidly than short rates. When conditions are deteriorating, owners at first hold out, so that the voyage rates fall more quickly than the time, and it is only later that the longer rates fall to a corresponding level.

---

[1] The explanation may have more plausibility than substance, as so many other factors were operating at the same time. The indices, too, should not be overstrained. The time charter market was very small during this period, as the liner companies took hardly any ships; in some months, as in June and July 1932 there were no quotations at all. [2] See footnote 4 on page 92.

II

INWARD AND OUTWARD RATES

Rates for voyages in one direction are traditionally said to move inversely to rates in the opposite direction; if the inward rate rises, the outward rate falls, and vice versa. We have now to examine the limitations of this tradition.

In the first place, if the cargo moving in one direction exceeds the cargo moving in the other, there will be some ships travelling in ballast. For instance, if outward cargoes are the smaller, some boats will be going out in ballast, and the outward rate will be at its minimum. If, then, the demand for ships inward increases, the inward rate may rise, but the outward rate cannot fall because it is already at its minimum. On the contrary it may well rise. Carrying an outward cargo involves delay; the ship has to unload at some port not necessarily the same as that at which the inward cargo is to be unloaded, and several days may be lost in this way. When charters are hard to get the loss of a few days does not matter much, but when business is booming the profit lost may be considerable, and a boat will only accept an outward cargo if it more than remunerates for lost time. It is therefore a common feature of the market for outward rates to rise simply because the inward rates have risen.[1]

Secondly, if there is a general rise of homeward rates on all routes, there is no reason why outward rates should fall. In a competitive market the rates between A and B are governed by the condition that a ship must be able to earn on the inward and outward voyages a profit per day equal to that which it could earn on inward and outward voyages between A and C. If the profit between A and C remains constant, then the profit on a round voyage between A and B is also given. Provided that ships are not moving in ballast, inward and outward rates between A and B will move inversely.[2] But if there is a general improvement

[1] For instance, in 1937 the increase in outward rates was "produced partly by the increase in coal exports from the United Kingdom of nearly 6,000,000 tons over 1936, and partly by the abundance of lucrative business obtainable homewards. Owners of the larger and more modern vessels, especially motor ships, could see satisfactory profits on a run out in ballast and home at the good rates offered, and would therefore not take coals out unless at tempting figures." "Angier's Shipping Report" in *Fairplay*, January 13, 1938.

[2] Not all voyages, of course, are round voyages; in fact it is quite common for a ship to do a "triangular" or "multilateral" voyage, wandering from port

in conditions—if the profit on a round voyage between A and C increases—then a rise in the rate from B to A need not be accompanied by any fall in the rate from A to B. Why should the owner take a lower rate to B because he can get a higher rate from B? The rate to B is governed by the cargo offering and the supply of ships. So long as conditions have improved on all routes, the increased rate from B need not be attracting any more ships to B, and consequently the rate to B need not fall. On the contrary, since the outward cargoes and inward cargoes usually rise together in boom years and fall together during the slump, we should expect inward rates and outward rates to rise and fall together.

There are therefore two tendencies at work in opposite directions. There is the tendency for inward and outward rates to move inversely on any one route when the general conditions elsewhere are stable; and there is the tendency for them to move together in the same direction when market conditions generally are changing. Costs also are important. Running costs tend to be high in the boom and low in the slump; and the secular trend of average costs is downwards because of technical progress. Costs affect both inward and outward voyages simultaneously, and raise or lower both rates together.

These tendencies can be observed in the available statistics. From 1923 to the outbreak of war in 1939 the *Economist* published a monthly index of inward and outward rates between Europe and South America, Europe and India, United Kingdom and the Mediterranean, and United Kingdom and Bay ports (Bilbao, Bordeaux), using the average of 1898 to 1913 as base.[1] In Charts II to V we have plotted these rates on scatter diagrams for the period 1923 to 1934. It will be seen that only in the case of South America is there a clear inverse relationship between the inward and

---

to port for many months before returning home. The effect of the existence of such voyages is to reduce the degree of fluctuation. Suppose, for example, that cargoes homeward from *B* to *A* increase. If all voyages were round voyages, all the additional ships required would have to come out from *A* to *B*, and the rate from *A* to *B* might be seriously depressed. But if some of the ships come to *B* from *C*, *D* and *E* the additional number required to go out to *B* from *A* is not so large and the outward rate is not depressed to the same extent. The more multilateral the voyage, the smaller, in the new equilibrium position, will be the rise in the inward rate and the fall in the outward rate. There will nevertheless be some inverse movement.

[1] For details as to the construction of these indices, see the *Economist, Monthly Supplement*, July 1923.

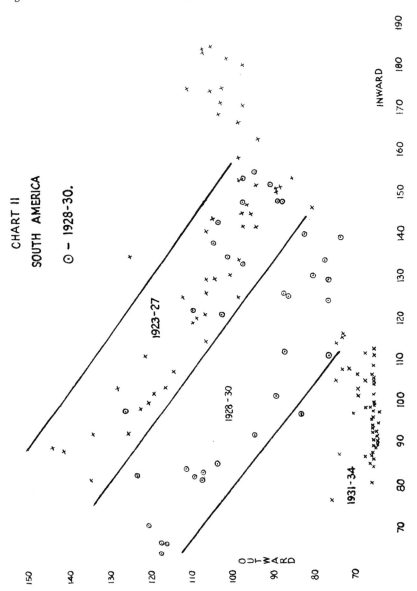

CHART II
SOUTH AMERICA
⊙ – 1928-30.

INWARD

1923-27

1928-30

1931-34

OUTWARD

outward rates. The Mediterranean and Bay show an even
more marked tendency for the rates to move in the same
direction.

In the case of South America the fact that the rates are not all

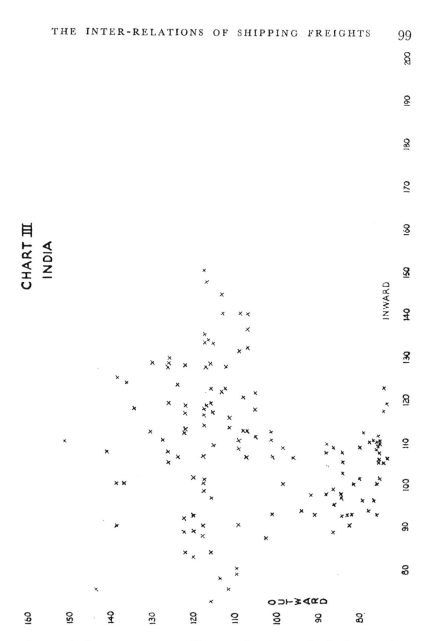

CHART III
INDIA

clustered along one narrow line moving inversely is due to the
tendency for the whole level of inward and outward rates to move
downwards in bad years and upwards in good years. Given fairly
stable conditions, however, inward and outward rates do move

inversely. The highest "band" of rates is that for the period 1923–27; except for a short period at the extreme right end of this band when inward and outward rates were falling together after the coal strike of 1926, rates moved inversely. Next comes the 1928–30 band, lower than that of 1923–27 because the decline

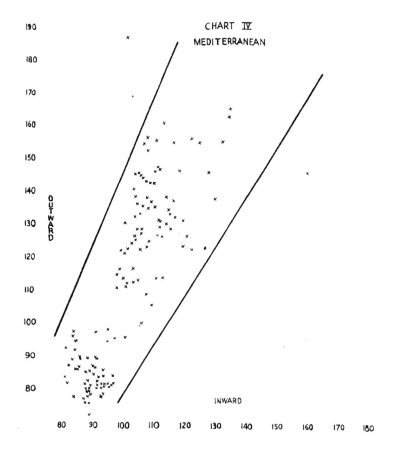

in coal exports led in all markets to a fall in the level of outward rates without any compensating rise in homeward rates. The correlation coefficient for 1923–29, taking percentage deviations from a twelve-monthly moving average is − 0·455 ± 0·070. Finally, in the period 1931–34 there is no inverse relationship; outward rates are at their minimum and do not respond to changes in inward rates. The seasonal fluctuations for the period 1923–34

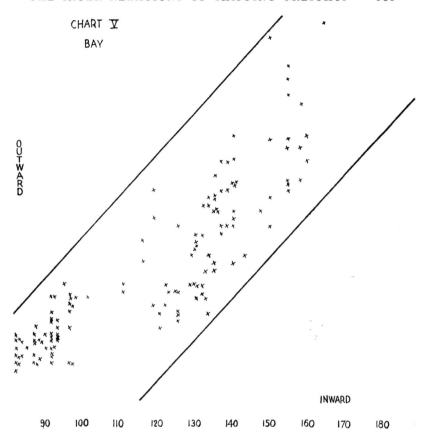

CHART V

BAY

OUTWARD

INWARD

90   100   110   120   130   140   150   160   170   180

(excluding 1926 when inward rates were abnormally affected by the coal strike) are as follows:

PERCENTAGE DEVIATIONS FROM THE TREND

	J	F	M	A	M	J	J	A	S	O	N	D
Inward	+8·2	+3·9	−0·5	+3·1	+1·1	−6·4	−3·8	−2·0	−5·3	−4·9	+0·1	+6·5
Outward	−4·7	−0·2	−0·6	−2·0	−0·2	+2·6	+0·6	−1·3	+5·2	+5·1	+0·7	−5·0

The inverse movement is clearly marked.[1]

[1] These seasonal figures and the correlation coefficient, being based on deviations from a twelve-monthly moving average, measure only the relations between seasonal and short-term fluctuations, and do not take account of cyclical and secular movements in the trend. Thus a negative correlation of deviations from the trend is not incompatible with a positive correlation of movements in the trend. Dr. Isserlis has been good enough to show me the results of his correlations of annual averages of inward and outward rates on many routes from 1869 to 1926. They are strongly positive, indicating that

The scatter diagram for India is not very informative, the only clear feature being the points at the bottom of the diagram which illustrate the principle that inward and outward rates move independently when the latter have reached their minimum level. Correlation technique is more helpful; indeed it is spectacular. For the whole period 1923–29 the coefficient is only — 0·199 ± 0·084. If, however, we break this period into two, 1923–27 and 1928–29, the first yields a strong negative coefficient of — 0·728 ± 0·054, and the second an equally strong positive coefficient of + 0·756 ± 0·059. That is to say, during the period 1923–27 inward and outward rates moved inversely, but during the next two years they moved together in the same direction, presumably because conditions were unsettled. The seasonal fluctuations for 1923–34 are as follows:

PERCENTAGE DEVIATIONS FROM THE TREND

	J	F	M	A	M	J	J	A	S	O	N	D
Inward	+6·9	+1·7	−1·0	−3·3	−4·5	−7·3	−5·3	−2·3	−0·9	+1·5	+5·2	+9·2
Outward	−2·1	−1·6	−0·9	−1·6	+0·2	+1·0	−0·6	+1·6	+1·2	+2·9	+0·2	−0·3

The outward fluctuation is small and the influence of the earlier years is sufficient to make it the reverse of the inward fluctuation.[1]

When we come to the Mediterranean and Bay the scatter diagrams leave no room for doubt that inward and outward rates in these waters move in the same direction. For the Mediterranean the correlation coefficient is + 0·532 ± 0·063. For the Bay it is + 0·410 ± 0·073. The seasonal fluctuations also confirm this.

PERCENTAGE DEVIATIONS FROM THE TREND

Mediterranean	J	F	M	A	M	J	J	A	S	O	N	D
Inward	+2·5	+1·9	+1·8	+1·3	−1·2	−2·7	−3·8	−3·6	−2·0	+0·2	+2·2	+3·3
Outward	−1·5	+0·3	+2·5	+1·5	+4·5	+3·6	−1·3	−3·6	−2·1	−1·3	−1·3	−1·4
Bay Inward	+2·4	+2·1	+0·5	−0·6	−1·2	−2·2	−2·5	−2·9	−2·4	+0·8	+2·3	+3·2
Outward	−0·3	−1·4	−3·3	−3·3	−2·8	−2·7	−1·5	−2·7	+0·6	+5·1	+7·5	+5·3

The explanation here seems to lie in the fact that the market for these routes is isolated from the market for ships for other routes, because the ships on these routes are small and unsuitable for long-distance ocean travel. Accordingly in the short period inward rates are independent of the outward. The outward rate is set by the volume of cargoes offered and the number of ships, and nothing that happens in the inward market affects either of

the secular and cyclical movement of these rates is in the same direction. This conclusion is quite to be expected, and not incompatible with the conclusion that month by month movements may be in opposite directions.

[1] It is not possible to use the indices for India with much confidence. There are so few outward freights to India that the outward index must be treated with reserve.

these two factors.[1] But since the general conditions which affect the market for inward cargoes also tend simultaneously to affect the market for outward cargoes, and in the same direction, it is not surprising to find inward and outward rates moving together.

The general conclusion of this section, therefore, must be that the relation between inward and outward rates is not a simple one. The traditional theory that the rates move inversely is adequate if (*a*) conditions are stable, (*b*) no ships are travelling in ballast, and (*c*) the route is not isolated from the market for other routes. Where any of these conditions is absent, inward and outward rates may move independently or in the same direction.

III

RATES ON DIFFERENT ROUTES

We have now to consider the relations between rates on different routes. What connection is there between rates between Australia and Europe, South America and Europe, South Africa and India, India and Europe, etc.?

In so far as a ship can transfer itself from one route to another, one should expect the governing condition to be that the profit which the marginal ship can earn on all routes must be the same. This, however, is true in the long run rather than the short. A sudden increase in demand for shipping at Port X will lead to a rise in freights for ships on the spot. This increase may last a few weeks until more ships arrive, bringing the rate into equilibrium with rates elsewhere. Rates on all routes need not move together month by month, but divergencies cannot long persist.

Accordingly round voyage rates (the sum of inward and outward rates) should move together in the same direction, but not necessarily to the same extent.[2] In the first place, ships are interchange-

---

[1] In the short run the number of ships is more or less fixed, though "ton-mileage" can be increased to a small extent by greater speed, quicker turn round, etc. In the long period more ships will be built if the round voyage yields abnormal profit, and this will tend to alter the relative level of rates to an extent depending on the relative elasticities of demand for shipping in each direction. Similarly, if the inward rate falls too low, some ships will be laid up, and this will tend to increase the outward rate (and vice versa).

[2] If a ship leaves port expecting to do not a round voyage but a multilateral voyage, then the condition is that the daily rate of profit on the voyage taken as a whole must not be less than could be secured on any other route. Some parts of the voyage may be abnormally profitable while others may even have to be done in ballast.

able as between routes only within limits. In general the ships of under 2,500 tons keep to the coasting trades and seldom do ocean voyages. The medium-sized ships keep to the American trades and others of similar distance. The largest ships are to be found on the Australian route. At the margin there are transferences. A certain ship may be indifferent as between a voyage from Cardiff to Alexandria or to the River Plate. Another may be indifferent between Australia and the Plate. The marginal ship must get the same profit on whichever route it sails, but the margin shifts. If the rates for long ocean voyages are doubled it does not follow that the rates on short coastal voyages will also be doubled, since the majority of the ships engaged on coastal voyages are not able to take advantage of the high ocean rates.

Again, the existence of out-of-pocket charges which are not the same for all routes affects the magnitude of the fluctuations. Compare for instance voyages on routes A to B and A to C, where ships on the C route must pass through a canal and pay a toll. If the rates on B route are doubled, it is not necessary for the rates on the C route to be doubled in order that ships should continue to be indifferent between the two routes. Suppose, for instance, that the two voyages are of equal length, that the out-of-pocket expenses on either voyage are £x, and canal dues on the C route £a. Then if the freight on the B route is £y, the freight on the C route must be £$y + a$. Then if the freight on the B route rises by 100 per cent to £$2y$, the freight on the C route need only rise to £$2y + a$, which is less than 100 per cent. The absolute increase must be the same, but not the relative increase. The significance of this point is that the rates for ships on routes with canals, such as the Indian route, or routes where port or other out-of-pocket expenses are above the average, should tend to fluctuate less than the rates on other routes. It means also that rates on long voyages should tend to fluctuate more than rates on short voyages; since the port charges do not vary with the length of the voyage, the average daily out-of-pocket expense is smaller on the long voyage than on the short, and rates should tend to fluctuate more widely. On the other hand, if the port charges are small, time spent in port is less costly than time spent at sea because fuel costs are small and there is less wear and tear. On short trips the ship spends a greater proportion of its time in port than it does on long voyages; where port charges are small the average daily out-of-pocket expense is less for the short voyage than for the long, and short rates should tend to fluctuate most; but cargoes which are expensive to handle may lead to the reverse conditions. Again, if there are differences in daily out-of-pocket expenses on different routes, then a rise of xd. per day in running costs (wages, coal, etc.) will call for a greater proportionate increase of freights on the voyages where the daily out-of-pocket expense is least. The influence of differences in daily average out-of-pocket expense is diverse. Some of the differences tend to make short voyage rates fluctuate most, others tend to make them fluctuate least.

If we had adequate statistics of round and multilateral voyages we might try to see what the net effect has been in the past. Unfortunately the available figures are confined to inward freights, and a few outwards. The position is not, however, hopeless, because we know that since the war of 1914–18 some ships have been moving outwards in ballast on all routes, and outward rates have tended to contribute little by way of gross profit. We can therefore use inward rates as a first approximation to an index of round voyage rates. The *Economist* index numbers of inward freights yield the following seasonal fluctuations for the period 1923–34 (excluding 1926 as before), calculated as percentage deviations from a twelve-monthly moving average. They are arranged in order of their standard deviation.

	J	F	M	A	M	J	J	A	S	O	N	D
Australia	+6·9	+2·2	−2·2	−4·2	−7·2	−10·1	−8·3	−3·0	+3·3	+7·1	+7·0	+8·1
India	+6·9	+1·7	−1·0	−3·3	−4·5	− 7·3	−5·3	−2·3	−0·9	+1·5	+5·2	+9·2
South America	+8·2	+3·9	−0·5	+3·1	+1·1	−6·4	−3·8	−2·0	−5·3	−4·9	+0·1	+6·5
Far East and Pacific	+5·8	+3·4	+0·9	+0·3	−2·9	− 5·2	−5·0	−3·5	−1·5	+1·2	+2·2	+4·8
North America	+1·3	+3·0	+0·8	+2·3	+1·1	− 4·0	−5·9	−4·2	−1·3	+0·9	+3·5	+2·5
Mediterranean	+2·5	+1·9	+1·8	+1·3	−1·2	− 2·7	−3·8	−3·6	−2·0	+0·2	+2·2	+3·3
Bay	+2·4	+2·1	+0·5	−0·6	−1·2	− 2·2	−2·5	−2·9	−2·4	+0·8	+2·3	+3·3

The standard deviations are as follows:

Australia	..	..	..	..	..	6·34
India ..	..	..	..	..	..	4·87
South America	..	..	..	..	4·54
Far East and Pacific ..	..	..	..	3·58
North America	..	..	..	..	3·00
Mediterranean	..	..	..	..	2·43
Bay ..	..	..	..	..	..	2·13

It will be seen that the shortest routes fluctuate least and the longest routes fluctuate most. This is all the more remarkable because rates on the longer routes might be expected to bear a similar relation to rates on the short routes to that which the long-term rate of interest bears to the short-term rate of interest. That is to say, the rates for long voyages should be a sort of average of the rates expected for short voyages during the next four or five months. In so far as seasonal fluctuations can be foreseen, the long rates should therefore fluctuate less than the short. That the reverse is the case suggests that the difference in out-of-pocket expenses is overwhelmingly in favour of the long routes. The evidence is not final, however, as inward freights are only a first approximation to what we are seeking. Outward freights tend to be more important on the short than on the long routes, while multilateral trips are more important on the long than on the short, and it is not clear how much allowance is to be made for these factors. Similar difficulties arise when we try to interpret the trend, which also shows differences in degree of fluctuation.

IV

THE CONTROL SCHEME

We have now completed our analysis of "normal" inter-relations. It remains to consider the effects of freight control by the Tramp Shipping Administrative Committee (hereinafter called T.S.A.C.) which commenced operations in February 1935.

T.S.A.C. was the outcome of the Government's decision to pay British tramp shipowners an annual subsidy of £2,000,000. The subsidy was to be based on the number of days actually spent on tramp voyages. Clearly if the market had remained competitive the bulk of the subsidy would have accrued to charterers since British shipowners would have competed with each other and with foreign shipowners and with the liner companies for the limited cargo available. Marginal costs would have fallen by the amount of the subsidy, and the market being competitive, freights would have fallen correspondingly. To use the language of the trade, the subsidy would have been "dissipated."

This result is not inherent in all forms of subsidy. The basis of the subsidy might have been not days spent on voyages, but number of days laid up. The "Tanker Pool" had already been functioning successfully for a year on this basis. If the British Government had adopted this basis for its subsidy, it would have helped to raise freights since the marginal cost of running a ship would have been increased by an amount equal to the subsidy forgone.[1] Or the subsidy might have been based on tonnage owned, whether employed or laid up. It would then have had little effect on freights in the short run, unless owners now offered their ships at less than marginal cost for sentimental or other reasons. To base the subsidy on tonnage employed made it necessary to have machinery for fixing minimum freights if the subsidy was not to be dissipated.

The Government's choice of this basis seems to have been due to its desire to increase the employment of British ships at the expense of foreign ships. But it was faced with a dilemma. The employment of British ships could be increased if British shipowners were enabled by the subsidy to undercut foreign shipowners; but if they did this the subsidy would be dissipated. In so far as shipowners kept the subsidy, they could not have more of their ships employed. Of course some British owners would now be able to recommission ships previously laid up, and there would be more British ships on the market waiting for the limited number of charters available, but if no undercutting were allowed, there would be only a slight increase in the chance that any ship chartered would be British. T.S.A.C. maintained in its Reports that though a minimum freight was established from the River Plate the subsidy helped British shipowners in that market at the expense of foreign shipowners, but the evidence it offers is not significant. British, Dutch and Jugoslav shipowners improved their position in 1935 at the expense of the Italians, who were busy around Abyssinia, and the Greeks, who were in difficulties over insurance. But in 1936 the British percentage was reduced as the Italians and the Greeks reappeared on the market.[2] The main effect of the subsidy was to increase the receipts of shipowners, and this could have been achieved even more effectively if the subsidy had

[1] For a description of the Tanker scheme and an analysis of its effect on freights see T. Koopmans, *Tanker Freight Rates and Tankship Building*. The British subsidy was actually distributed in such a way that owners with tonnage laid up got a slightly higher subsidy per ton employed than owners with less or no tonnage laid up; but there is no reason to believe that the difference was significant; see "A Baltic Broker's Log" in the *Shipping World*, September 18, 1935.

[2] T.S.A.C. issued six half-yearly reports which were published as white papers. For 1935 see Cmds. 5004 and 5084; for 1936, Cmds. 5291 and 5363; for 1937, Cmds. 5555 and 5750. No reports were issued for 1938 or 1939.

been based not on tons employed but on tons owned or tons laid up.[1]

T.S.A.C. was born of the subsidy, but it was not an official body, and it survived the subsidy. In 1935 and 1936 British shipowners were encouraged to support it because they would have forfeited the subsidy if they had not. 1937 was a boom year, during which market rates were above the minima laid down by T.S.A.C. anyway. The real test of T.S.A.C.'s authority came in 1938 and 1939, during which its minimum rates were well above the market level, and no subsidy was payable. The respect paid to T.S.A.C.'s authority both by British and by foreign shipowners in this critical period when it had no power to enforce sanctions surprised all who had argued that tramp shipowners could not voluntarily be associated in a price-fixing scheme.

This is not to say that there was 100 per cent loyalty. A scheme fixing minimum rates outwards to the St. Lawrence and United States was wrecked by the disloyalty of foreign shipowners. This scheme was originally in two parts: coals from United Kingdom and Baltic ports, and coals from Black Sea ports. The principal charterer in the latter market was the Soviet Government. This Government maintained a firm opposition to the "capitalist monopoly" and exerted its utmost influence to get foreign shipowners to ignore it. It was so successful that the Black Sea scheme was withdrawn in April 1936, after a short life of only five months.

[1] Dr. Isserlis comments: "There was an apparent inconsistency in the double object of (a) not dissipating the subsidy and (b) improving the employment of British tramp shipping. By the introduction of minimum freight rate schemes and the, in the main, wholehearted co-operation of Greek and Norwegian shipowners, the two objects were achieved during the period of low freights lasting from 1935 to the autumn of 1936. Such difficulties as occurred were due less to the failure to secure 100 per cent willingness to co-operate than to two factors not referred to by you. The first was the habit, before 1935, of certain British and Norwegian shipowners to enter into long-period contracts with charterers. They were not long-period time charters, but contracts to lift a certain amount of cargo per year for some years ahead. The second was that the co-operation of German tramp and liner owners was formal only. Any owner, British or foreign, was under compulsion to carry out the instructions of the T.S.A.C. only if he were free to do so. Orders from his own Government to do something else relieved him from the obligation. On many occasions when British, Greek and Norwegian shipowners obeyed instructions not to proceed in ballast to the Plate, German tramp ships were loading homeward grain cargoes steadily although 50 or 70 British and other tramp ships had been waiting in the River Plate for weeks. The explanation was that these were German Government cargoes."

The Black Sea and United Kingdom scheme continued, despite some undercutting by Scandinavian owners, but when in November 1936 the Canadian Government removed the prohibition of anthracite imports from Russia, this half of the scheme had also to be dropped. Russian opposition also wrecked another scheme, commended but not fathered by T.S.A.C., covering the Baltic timber trade. First started in 1935, this scheme had to be discontinued after a few months; and when revived in 1938 it met a similar fate.

In the case of T.S.A.C.'s other schemes foreign co-operation was very good until March 1939. Foreign shipowners were represented on T.S.A.C., and complaints of evasion were few. In 1938 and 1939, however, business in the River Plate was very bad, owing to the poor grain crops, and as the minimum rate in force was considered fairly high, the loyalty of shipowners was severely strained. It broke in March 1939 when a batch of Greek fixtures was suddenly reported, at rates believed to be well below the minimum rate. T.S.A.C. immediately responded by reducing the minimum rate by 20 per cent, and the Greek Government kindly passed legislation to compel Greek owners to observe the minimum rates. With the exception of this lapse the schemes held together very well indeed.

T.S.A.C.'s work raised many interesting problems into which we cannot enter here. There was the problem of deciding adequate differentials for large ships and small ships, for whole cargoes and for berth and liner parcel business. Then there was the problem of making sure that on each route all competing ports were included; Newcastle, New South Wales, had to be included in the Australian scheme after twenty months; the control of grain freights from the St. Lawrence was extended from time to time until it included all United States eastern ports and the Gulf. There were also minor methods of evasion, such as allowing the charterer to do his own stevedoring, varying the rate for "two-port options," chartering simultaneously a ship on a regulated and a ship on an unregulated route, the latter at less than the ruling market rate, and so on. There is in T.S.A.C.'s experience much material for students of the technique of market control. But we must confine ourselves in this chapter to one topic, namely the effect of rates which were controlled on those which were not controlled. T.S.A.C. did not fix minimum rates for all trades; grain freights from the River Plate, from Australia and from North

American ports were controlled; the others were left to find their own level in the market. It is interesting and important to know what effect these controlled freights, the most important in the market, had on uncontrolled freights, and to this problem we now turn.

V

EFFECTS OF CONTROL

We can begin by dismissing two opposite theories. The first is the suggestion that raising freights on some routes must tend to depress freights on the others since boats unable to find cargoes on the regulated routes will crowd into the unregulated and depress freights there. For this to be the case, it must be shown that the volume of trade on the regulated routes would be greater if freights were lower. Shipowners are almost unanimous in the opinion that the elasticity of demand is zero. It may make some difference, as between grain moving from the Plate, Australia, or North America, what relation exists between the freights from those ports. But provided that the proper relationship is maintained, there is little reason to believe that a general fall in grain freights from all ports would have any significant effect on the volume of trade in grain. This contention may seem to be disproved by the events of March 1939. Throughout 1938 the minimum rate for grain from the Plate was fixed at 25s. Charterers maintained that the rate was too high. They held off chartering, going as it were on strike; and eventually found some Greek ships to undercut the minimum rate. T.S.A.C. was beaten; the rate was forthwith lowered to 20s. and an astonishing amount of chartering occurred. But this does not prove that elasticity of demand was greater than zero. All that happened was a transference of demand in time; in a few weeks business relapsed. Had T.S.A.C. been able to hold out, the charterers would sooner or later have had to give in, and the volume of business done at 25s. would not have differed materially from the volume done at 20s. If this is so, the minimum freights on some routes cannot be said to exercise a depressing influence on other routes, for the number of ships seeking cargo on those routes is not increased.

The other argument postulates that freights on the unregulated routes must come up to the level of freights on the regulated routes since no owner will accept a low rate on an unregulated route when he can get a higher freight on a regulated route. This would be the case if charterers were prepared to take an unlimited number of ships on the regulated routes at the minimum rate. If on the other hand there were no business at all to be done on the regulated routes, owners would have to accept whatever rate they could get on the unregulated routes. The argument that freights must rise all round if some "key" freights are increased by T.S.A.C. is too simple to be accepted, and was in fact belied by the events.

Examination of this argument, however, points to the correct solution: the effect of the minimum freights depends on the volume of business available on regulated routes. If these routes are able to absorb unlimited tonnage at the minimum freight, freights on other routes must rise to the level of the regulated routes. If no business is doing at the minimum freights, they have no effect. The volume of business is the key to the situation.

The volume of business on the regulated routes is important because it determines how long a ship arriving at a regulated port will have to wait for a cargo. The cost of waiting in the Plate for a cargo was estimated in March 1938 at about 6d. per ton per week.[1] The minimum rate was 25s. per ton. We can therefore say, as a rough first approximation, that if the owner were offered 16s. for some other journey of equivalent length and cost, he could afford to refuse it if he thought he could get a cargo from the Plate by waiting there less than eighteen weeks, but would accept it if he expected a longer wait.

The Plate is now the principal tramp trade, and long waits there were the rule during 1935, 1936, 1938 and 1939 (1937 was a boom year). At one time there were seventy vessels waiting. From the beginning of the scheme T.S.A.C. found it necessary to restrict sailings to the Plate for fear that a heavy accumulation of tonnage there would cause the scheme to collapse. Vessels were forbidden from March 1935 to proceed to the Plate in ballast without first having obtained a fixture. This did not stop ships from proceeding with outward cargoes, and such ships accumulated waiting for fixtures. Accordingly in March 1936 ships were forbidden to sail from the Plate in ballast even if they could first obtain a fixture; the plums were to be reserved for such ships as could get outward cargoes. Tonnage with outward cargoes nevertheless accumulated, so in June 1936 even ships proceeding outward with cargoes were prohibited from accepting fixtures until such time as T.S.A.C. should determine. These restrictions were

[1] "A Baltic Broker's Log" in the *Shipping World*, March 9, 1938.

gradually relaxed as business improved in the second half of the year, but they had to be reimposed in 1938 and 1939 when the boom of 1937 had ended. Their effect was to compel each ship entering the Plate to take its turn in the queue. Owners could estimate how long they would have to stay in the queue, and calculate accordingly in deciding what minimum rate would be acceptable in unregulated trades. The effect of this principle is clearly marked in the indices of unregulated freights. They fell in the first half of 1935, of 1936 and of 1938 despite the existence of minimum freights elsewhere, and they revived at the end of 1936 and in the second quarter of 1939 when business conditions improved in regulated trades.

A similar principle can be applied to explain the effect of the regulation of homeward rates upon the unregulated outward rates; the longer the ship expects to have to wait for a homeward cargo, the higher the freight it will demand for the outward journey. This was particularly noticeable in the early half of 1938; homeward prospects from the Plate were deteriorating, and the outward rate rose steadily from about 9s. in January to 16s. in March to compensate for the long period of waiting for a homeward cargo. Outward rates were also affected by T.S.A.C.'s restrictions on sailings. In those periods when ships were forbidden to move outwards in ballast, an outward cargo was a "passport" to the Plate, and outward rates declined; this happened in March 1936, and again in November 1937, when its immediate effect was to reduce the outward rate from 11s. 9d. to 9s. The reverse happened when T.S.A.C. forbade even ships with an outward cargo to fix homeward from the Plate, as in June 1936 and March 1938. On the former occasion the rate jumped from 8s. 3d. to 12s., but fell again as the market realised that the restriction only added a little to the probable wait in the Plate. To sum up, the effect of fixing a minimum rate is that outward freights no longer move inversely. The inward rate is pegged. The outward falls if prospects improve, or if restrictions are placed on ballast sailings. It rises if prospects homeward deteriorate, and especially if vessels carrying cargoes are compelled to join a queue for inward cargoes.

Lastly, time charter rates. As these were not fixed by T.S.A.C. there was an obvious loophole for evading the minimum voyage charter rates. From the start it was expected that speculators would hire ships on time charter and re-let them on voyage charter at less than minimum rates; such speculators, not being shipowners, owed no loyalty to T.S.A.C. Accordingly the Committee ruled shortly after the schemes were inaugurated that shipowners when hiring on time charter must stipulate that the vessel should comply with all the conditions of minimum freight schemes if used on any of the routes to which such schemes applied.

This ruled out speculators, but it did not touch the merchant hiring a ship for his own use. When business prospects were bad, ships could be offered on time charter at the true market rate, which was much below the minimum rate. A clear case occurred in the St. Lawrence trade in November 1936, and T.S.A.C. met it immediately by ruling that time charters must in future provide that the ship should not be used to carry grain from the St. Lawrence. This provision was, however, withdrawn in 1937 when conditions improved.

In 1938 the difficulty arose again. Six ships were taken on time charter in May to carry grain from the Argentine. T.S.A.C. then ruled that no ship should be let on time charter for any period commencing with the voyage homeward from the Argentine. This provision was subsequently extended to the other regulated routes as well. It was, however, not sufficient since it could be evaded by starting the time charter with an outward voyage. A ruling in July expressed the vain hope that ships would not be let on time charter at a rate less than the equivalent minimum voyage rate. Finally, in February 1939 T.S.A.C. was driven to rule that every time charter must contain a provision prohibiting the ship from loading in the Argentine. The time charter rate reflected the true market position. If the voyage rate was to be fixed, T.S.A.C. had either to fix the time charter rate as well or to banish time-chartered ships from the regulated routes. It chose the latter course.

VI
CONCLUSION

It may be thought that T.S.A.C. might have made its control of freights more effective by fixing not just some rates but all of them. The difficulties in the way of doing this were enormous. Even the limited control produced its problems. Thus, tonnage accumulated abnormally in the Plate during 1938 and early 1939 because the minimum rate there was too high relatively to the minimum rates elsewhere and to the unregulated rates. A simple ruling that the rate on each route was to be the equivalent of xd.

per ton per day would have overcome this sort of difficulty, but not others. As we have seen in the first part of this paper, there is no simple relationship between the various rates. Time charter rates for short periods are sometimes above and sometimes below rates for longer periods; and in addition the rate for each ship is different, depending on its speed, fuel consumption, etc.[1] Inward and outward rates move sometimes together and sometimes inversely. Rates on different routes must fluctuate in different degrees because of differences in costs. Doubtless it would not be beyond human ingenuity to vary the relations between minimum rates week by week so as to take account of the changing conditions which require rates to diverge from each other. But the task would call for a more extensive machinery and more intimate knowledge of fluctuating conditions than is normally to be expected. Even as it was, T.S.A.C., though controlling only a limited number of rates, had to appeal from time to time for detailed returns from shipowners on which to base its decisions. Complete freight control is a gigantic task if the proper inter-relations of freights are not to be disregarded.

Finally, it is on the divergencies of some rates from other rates that the world depends for a proper distribution of ships in the different parts of the globe. If cargoes at A increase, the rate there rises and ships are attracted; if cargoes diminish the rate falls and ships are encouraged to move elsewhere. If rates are all fixed this mechanism for controlling the flow of shipping ceases to function, and must be replaced by some authoritarian method of getting the right ships in the right places at the right times. This can be seen with inland transport. Railway rates are more or less stable. An increase in traffic from A is not accompanied by an increased rate attracting more trains. But since the railway company is under a statutory obligation to carry all traffic offered to it, the additional trains are secured without any change in the rate. If shipping freights are to be stabilised, there must be some such law, and an authority capable of enforcing it. And since shipping is international, it would have to be an international law, administered by an international body with full powers to order ships hither and thither.

[1] Wartime requisitioning of ships on time charter illustrates the objection to fixing a uniform time charter rate. The fixed rate of hire for requisitioned ships at present in force does no justice to the more modern, economical, well-equipped vessel.

T.S.A.C. avoided these problems by fixing a limited number of rates and leaving the others to adjust themselves in the market. Within this limited field it was eminently successful. It prevented the subsidy from being "dissipated" in the regulated trades, and though it probably had little effect on its dissipation in unregulated trades, or on the level of rates there while conditions were at their worst, it certainly maintained rates in some of the principal tramp trades, and hastened the rise of rates elsewhere when business prospects improved.

CHAPTER V

COMPETITION IN RETAIL TRADE

"The prejudices of some political writers against shopkeepers and tradesmen are altogether without foundation. So far from it being necessary either to tax them or to reduce their number, they can never be multiplied so as to hurt the public though they may be so as to hurt one another. The quantity of grocery goods, for example, which can be sold in a particular town, is limited by the demand of that town and its neighbourhood. The capital, therefore, which can be employed in the grocery trade, cannot exceed what is sufficient to purchase that quantity. If this capital is divided between two different grocers, their competition will tend to make both of them sell cheaper than if it was in the hands of one only; and if it were divided among twenty, their competition would be just so much the greater and the chance of their combining together, in order to raise the price, just so much the less. Their competition might, perhaps, ruin some of themselves; but to take care of this is the business of the parties concerned, and may be safely left to their own discretion."

Thus spake the old master in 1776.[1] His conclusion has never been widely accepted. Retailers have always claimed that competition hurts the public no less than themselves and sought public support for their elaborate efforts to restrain it. Even the classical writers were unsure.[2] Modern economists feel more confident to tackle the problem, using as tools the newly shaped theory of monopolistic competition, but a combined knowledge of theory and of the structure of retailing is all too rare, and attempts at a synthesis all too infrequent. A further venture does not therefore seem superfluous. Neither is the moment untimely. In November 1941 the Board of Trade made an Order prohibiting any person from opening a new retail business in this country except under licence. This was purely a wartime measure, and the President of the Board pledged himself to withdraw it after the war. But its enactment raised some hopes that permanent restrictions would

---

[1] Smith, A.: *The Wealth of Nations* (Cannan's Edition), Vol. I, pp. 341–2.
[2] Cf. the extracts from the classical economists gathered together in H. Smith, *Retail Distribution*, Ch. IV.

follow, and recent fortunes at the polls have helped to revive these hopes. Meanwhile, some town planning authorities are already using, or planning to use, their powers in such a way as drastically to reduce the number of shops. This article may, perhaps, help to clarify the issues involved.

The procedure adopted is to analyse first the effects of competition in prices and in services. The third section deals with certain special forms of competition which have been denounced as unfair, and the fourth section tries to reach conclusions on the main issues in the debate.

I

THE NUMBER, SIZE AND LOCATION OF SHOPS

1. In the contemporary approach, the earliest doubts of the effectiveness of competition in retailing are associated with the name of Hotelling. In a stimulating article[1] he argued, on certain special assumptions, that the effect of competition would be to cause sellers to cluster together, instead of dispersing at equal distances, and showed that this undesirable result in location causes transport costs to be excessive. Various writers interested themselves in the problem, but the outstanding advance is the contribution of Lerner and Singer eight years later, in an article[2] which generalises Hotelling's case, and is the most convenient starting point.

The basic assumption is that the customers are strung out at equal distances along a road. Then, on the further asumptions (a) that no two shops can be on the same spot; (b) that each end of the road is a cul-de-sac; (c) that each customer pays his own transport costs; (d) that the number of shops is given; (e) that the price is fixed; and (f) that there are no economies of scale, Lerner and Singer show that in equilibrium (i) there cannot be more than two shops together, and (ii) there must be two shops together at each end of the road. They also imply that each shop must have the same number of customers, unless there is an odd number of shops, when one may have more than the others; but this is not so. The third condition of equilibrium is only that no shop may have less customers than half the number between any two other shops, or less than the shops at the end. Shops may be

---

[1] Hotelling, H.: "Stability in Competition," *Economical Journal*, June 1929.
[2] A. P. Lerner, and H. W. Singer, "Some Notes on Duopoly and Spatial Competition," *Journal of Political Economy*, April 1937.

equidistant, but need not be, and as in any case the end shops must be paired, transport costs must be above the ideal.

Removing some of these assumptions brings the equilibrium conditions nearer to the ideal. Assumption (*a*) makes a negligible difference. Removing assumption (*b*) destroys conclusion (ii); if the road connects say two big market centres, the first shop at either end of the road may stand alone. As for assumption (*c*), Lerner and Singer themselves reach the important conclusion that if transport costs are paid not by the customers but by the sellers, shops will be located at equal distances from each other, which is the ideal situation.

2. To advance the analysis beyond the Lerner-Singer stage it is necessary to remove the remaining assumptions. If the number of shops is not given, and prices are not fixed, and there are no economies of scale, the number of shops will be as great as the number of customers. This odd conclusion brings into the open the odd assumption underlying the whole analysis that transport cost from wholesaler to retailer can be neglected, but not transport cost from retailer to customer, an assumption which becomes the more unreasonable the greater the ratio of shops to customers. Nevertheless, the conclusion serves to remind us that the convenience of customers requires that there should be as many shops as possible, each small, and that it is only economies of scale which prevent this. The assumption of constant costs is incompatible with equilibrium in retailing, given dispersal of customers. For if a reduction in the size of shops will not increase costs, it will pay some seller to insert himself between two existing shops.

Should shops, then, be of "optimum" size, meaning the minimum size consistent with minimum average cost, or should they be smaller, and if so, how much smaller? If we can assume that the inconvenience of not having a shop nearby can be translated into monetary terms as a function of the distance of the shop, the problem is capable of precise solution.

Let us assume (1) that all shops have the same costs; (2) that there are no prime costs, but only an overhead, so that the average cost curve is a rectangular hyperbola (marginal costs are assumed away only for convenience of exposition; what matters is the assumption of falling average cost); (3) that the customers are strung out along a road on either side of each shop, one customer for each unit of distance; (4) that each customer buys one unit (money value) of merchandise; and (5) that the inconvenience of distance can be expressed as one unit of money per unit of distance, paid by the customer. Then the following diagram shows the position.

AC is a rectangular hyperbola, representing the average cost curve of any shop, varying with the number of its customers (and therefore sales). MTC is the curve of marginal transport costs; the first two customers, one on either side, incur one unit each, the next two customers incur two units each, and so on; the curve can thus be drawn for simplicity as a straight line with a slope of 0·5. Total transport cost is the area lying beneath it, and average transport cost per customer will be a line with a slope of 0·25.

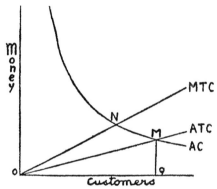

The ideal number of shops (or number of customers per shop) is such that, given the total number of customers to be served, the sum of shop costs and transport costs is at its minimum. This condition is fulfilled when for each shop the sum of average shop costs and average transport costs is minimised. Since for each new customer the former falls and the latter rises, the condition is fulfilled when the negative slope of AC equals the positive slope of ATC. AC being a rectangular hyperbola and ATC a straight line from the origin, this will be at the point where they meet. M gives us the ideal size of shop. It cannot correspond with the point where average shop cost would be minimised; since ATC is rising and AC is falling, the minimum point of ATC + AC must be to the left of the minimum point of AC. In other words, it is desirable that shops should be of less than "optimum" size.

Will competition bring about the right size? If there is free entry, and if there cannot be abnormal profits, the price charged by each shop (its gross margin) must lie somewhere along AC. If a shop reduces its price by one unit it will attract two customers, one on either side, who transfer their custom from its rivals. It pays therefore to lower the price by one unit if getting two more customers will reduce AC by more than one unit. Its equilibrium is therefore at the point N where the slope of MTC equals the slope of AC.[1] Thus shops will not cut their prices low enough to bring the right size. In competition, there will be too many shops, each too small.

The result can be generalised by assuming that consumers do not live along a road, but are distributed over an area, one in each unit of space. It remains desirable that shops should be

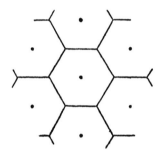

equidistant, and this condition can only be fulfilled if each is at the centre of a hexagon. How many shops there should be, and what should be the size of each, is then determined if we know how large the hexagon should be. Retaining our previous assumptions, the solution is as follows: If we write r for the length of the radius of the inscribed circle, the length of each side will be $1 \cdot 15r$. The number of customers equals the area of the hexagon, $3 \cdot 46r^2$. Writing a for the overhead costs of each shop, average cost per customer,

$$\mathrm{AC} = \frac{a}{3 \cdot 46r^2}.$$

To calculate transport costs we first divide the hexagon into its twelve right-angled triangles. In each, taking the customers living along the base, the nearest lives at distance r and the furthest at

[1] N corresponds to Chamberlin's "ideal adjustment" and to R in Fig. 15 of his *Theory of Monopolistic Competition*, p. 92. The slope of *MTC* here corresponds to the slope of dd^1 in that diagram.

distance $1\cdot15r$. The sum[1] of the distances for the base customers is $0\cdot61r^2$, and the total transport cost for the hexagon is twelve times the integral of this, i.e. $2\cdot41r^3$. This divided by the number of customers gives average transport cost per customer,

$$\text{ATC} = 0\cdot70r.$$

The ideal number of shops is given by the condition that the slopes of AC and ATC must be the same. Differentiating gives

$$\frac{a}{1\cdot73r^3} = 0\cdot70$$

$$\therefore r = 0\cdot93a^{\frac{1}{3}}.$$

Now, in competition a shop will cut its price by one unit so long as the resulting increase of customers reduces AC by more than one unit. Equilibrium therefore results when

$$\frac{a}{1\cdot73r^3} = 1$$

$$\therefore r = 0\cdot83a^{\frac{1}{3}}.$$

This analysis brings out the relevant points. The number of shops depends on the extent of the economies of scale, the density of population (determining the number of customers per unit of distance), and the inconvenience or cost of distant shopping. The greater the economies of scale, and the less the cost of transport, the fewer shops there will and should be. The denser the population, the larger shops will be, and this is worth noting since many people believe that the decentralisation of urban populations which has occurred since 1920 is one of the principal factors explaining the increase in the numbers engaged in distribution in this country.[2] In any case, given the dispersion of customers, the ideal size of shop is less than the "optimum"; and, given competition, the actual size will be less than the ideal.[3]

[1] I am indebted to Professor R. G. D. Allen for the formula.

[2] E.g. P. Ford, "Changes in the Number of Shops, 1901–1931," *Economic Journal*, June 1936.

[3] The above example assumed that goods are transported as the crow flies. More realistic assumptions do not upset the argument unless immensely complicated routes have to be used. For example, if we assume that main roads run direct from shop to shop, and that side roads are perpendicular to these main roads at intervals of one unit, total transport cost becomes $2\cdot98r^3$; the optimum number of shops will be given by the equation $r = 0\cdot88a^{\frac{1}{3}}$, and the competitive number remains at $r = 0\cdot83a^{\frac{1}{3}}$.

3. Several qualifications are needed before we can derive from this anything like a complete picture.

First, the analysis has so far assumed that there is price competition, and that each shop cuts prices without taking the reaction of its competitors into account. This does not require that the price of every one of the hundreds of commodities it sells should be keenly competitive; it is enough that average gross margins for any class of trade must be adjusted to the level set by competition, and if this is so, the effect on size is the same. But even this is not a complete picture. To begin with, retail prices in certain trades—cigarettes, patent medicines, some groceries, milk, coal, confectionery, books, periodicals, stationery, lamps, cycles, petrol, motors and motor accessories—are maintained by elaborate arrangements between manufacturers, wholesalers and retailers, which impose heavy penalties for price cutting. The assumption that retailers are free to compete in prices, however, holds good in other trades—some groceries, fish, meat, fruit and vegetables, flowers, furniture, most hardware, drapery, footwear, clothes, pottery and others—and to these the analysis applies, subject to further qualifications.

When prices are fixed the number of shops is a direct function of the level at which they are fixed. In terms of Fig. III (which is constructed on the same cost assumptions as Fig. I), equilibrium is given by the point K at which the horizontal price line SP cuts AC. So long as shops are larger than this they will be making profits; new entrants will then be attracted, reducing the share of each in the trade, until abnormal profits vanish. As the price is usually too high under these schemes (for reasons we shall examine later) the number of shops will be excessive. At this point, however, it will pay any one shop to compete by offering better service. If all shops do this, as they must in competition, all make losses unless their number contracts, and in competition it will contract up to the point where a curve showing the effect on sales of increased expenditure on service has the same slope as the new cost curve (including the additional services). In Fig. III we assume that the cost of the extra services is added not to marginal cost but to overheads; and we also assume that to increase the quality of the service at a cost of xd. per unit of sales has the same effect in stimulating sales as would reducing the price by xd. per unit while keeping the service unchanged. Competitive equilibrium is then given by the intersection of MTC and the fixed price line, to which the number of shops (and AC + S) adjusts itself. Where the extra services take the form of an addition to overhead costs, shops will be larger than they would be if there were competition in price but not in service, but prices will be higher. If they take the form of an addition to marginal costs, shops may be larger or smaller, higher or rising marginal costs making for smaller shops.

Shops may, of course, compete neither in prices nor in service, even though prices are not maintained. If each shopkeeper takes into account the fact that if he cuts prices or offers more service his rivals will follow, shops will be still smaller and more numerous.

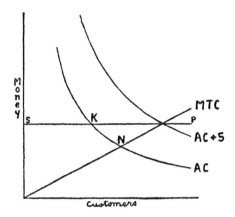

The limit to their smallness will be set by the elasticity of demand in the market as a whole, i.e. by Q in Chamberlin's Fig. 15[1]; in our diagram where elasticity is assumed to be zero it would be one shop for each customer. It is most unlikely in practice that this movement towards the upper limit will get very far. It is certainly unlikely in the United States of America, where aggressive competition is the rule, with chains, super-markets and independents at each other's throats. Competition is not so keen in this country, but competition between the co-operatives, the multiples and the independents is nevertheless keen enough in non-price-maintained trades to keep the size of shops near to N. In the price-maintained trades price competition is ruled out; service competition tends to check the decrease in shop size, but it is not always very strong and, given the fall in wholesale prices

[1] Loc. cit., p. 92.

which had been occurring steadily after 1920, it was possible for more and more redundant shops to establish themselves on an ever-widening gross margin.

4. The second qualification concerns transport costs. The conclusion that in competition there must be too many shops depends on the assumption that customers pay transport costs. If the shop pays transport costs, it will take on an extra customer so long as the price exceeds the cost of transporting to him (marginal selling cost being on our assumptions zero). But since (Fig. I) MTC equals the price (AC + ATC) at the point where AC + ATC is at its minimum, it follows that the point of equilibrium for the shop paying transport costs is the same as the ideal equilibrium, represented by the output OQ. There will be too many shops if customers pay their own transport costs, but the ideal number of shops if there is free delivery.

The reason for this is that free delivery is a form of price discrimination (in this case perfect discrimination), and, if average costs are falling, discrimination usually brings output nearer to the ideal. The discrimination arises because the nearest customers pay a price in excess of AC plus the cost of transporting to them, and the furthest pay the same price which is much below AC plus the cost of transporting to them (indeed the furthest customer contributes nothing towards AC); in a sense the nearer subsidise the further. The same sort of result would be attained by any other form of discrimination, and is not the result of competition in service as such. If all the customers get as much service as they pay for, the result is merely to lift the average cost curve; shops may be larger, but the gap between the ideal and the competitive equilibrium is not diminished. However, there are also forms of service other than delivery which involve discrimination, e.g. credit and subsidised restaurants in department stores. Whenever a service is paid for by some who do not use it, and used by some *who would buy elsewhere but for this service*, the effect is to bring the competitive equilbrium nearer to the ideal equilibrium.

We must also note precisely what transport cost means in this context. MTC is a measure of all the inconvenience associated with buying at a distant shop. It is not the same as what it would cost the shop in money to deliver one's purchases. A customer who shops in the centre of the town may be quite capable of carrying home a pair of shoes without much extra trouble or inconvenience, and if asked to pay an extra sum equal to what delivery would cost the shop, might prefer to carry for himself. When, therefore, one concludes that shops will be larger and of optimum size if they offer free delivery but not otherwise, one concludes too much. If the firm's transport costs exceed the value of the real convenience conferred on the customer, the shop will not reach optimum size even if there is free delivery, and may indeed be smaller than it would be without free delivery if the disparity is great.

5. The third qualification is to remove the assumption of zero elasticity of demand. It will be more profitable for the shopkeeper to lower his price if he can count on selling more to his existing customers as well as on attracting other people's customers, so an elasticity exceeding zero will bring the competitive number of shops nearer to the ideal number, or even below it. There may be no "excess capacity" if elasticity is large enough. Of the many modifications elasticity introduces into the results, this is the important one.

6. Next we must consider the assumption that there cannot be abnormal profits in equilibrium. This rests on two further assumptions. The first is that customers have no irrational preferences for shops, so that if two shops differ in nothing but their average price levels, customers will always buy from the cheaper. There has been some attempt to explain retailing, using as a large element in the analysis the irrationality, ignorance and inertia of customers.[1] While it is impossible to deny that these factors have some importance, it is impossible to agree to any significant importance in view of the rapid changes constantly taking place in the structure of retailing, as reflected in the relative strengths of independents, multiples, department stores, street markets, and the co-operative societies. Any shopkeeper who used the irrationality, ignorance, or inertia of his customers as major elements in his policy would soon find himself in Carey Street.

The other assumption necessary to keep prices equal to average cost is that continuous variability in the number of customers per shop is possible in each locality. This cannot be taken for granted. In the suburbs a new shop sets up between two other shops, and its impact is borne more heavily by the sales of these shops than it is by the sales of other shops. At any given moment, therefore, with a given number of shops, it may be that if a new shop could

[1] See especially H. Smith: op. cit., Ch. V.

be introduced in such a way as to take trade away equally from all shops (i.e. if all the shops were re-located at shorter intervals and one added), the new shop could remain permanently, but that since it would in fact be limited to sharing in the trade of two or three others, the shop will not be established. Certain consequences flow. First, profits may be abnormal without new shops being established, because there is more than enough for two but not enough for three; the corollary is that shops may be larger and fewer than the true competitive equilibrium. On the other hand, if too many shops come into existence, there is less likelihood of price or service competition, because in a small market sellers are more likely to take account of each other's reactions; and the entry of a new shop results simply in higher prices. There is, however, a check on this. Suburban shops compete not only with each other but also with shops in the large shopping centres, which are more aggressive. This fact makes possible continuous variability; it prevents suburban shopkeepers from exploiting a local monopoly, and keeps down the number of shops.

7. The fifth qualification is now to take full account of the existence of these large shopping centres.

From the analytical point of view, the difference is that we remove the assumptions that the customers are strung out evenly, one in each spot, and that transport costs are involved. For at a shopping centre there are thousands of persons who find themselves there for reasons other than shopping, and who, once there, can shop without counting transport cost. If we remove the assumption of transport costs, and assume large enough numbers of customers, it follows that in a large shopping centre shops should be of "optimum" size, meaning that average cost is at a minimum. The customer in Oxford Street takes real feminine pleasure in shopping; she moves around comparing prices and qualities, consulting her friends, and taking hours (or days) to make up her mind. It would be too much to claim that elasticity of demand is infinite for each shop, especially in the naïve sense that a small shaving of price immediately expands sales; but it is not too much to say that, in trades where the customer shops around, shops with cheap prices will sooner or later bankrupt those which try to sell similar qualities with similar service at a higher price level in the same centre. In the long run, therefore, shops in large shopping centres must approximate to optimum size.

This conclusion at once explains two common phenomena. First that shops in the centre are usually larger than those in the suburbs, and secondly that their prices are in consequence frequently lower[1]; and it reinforces the point that the suburban shop has only a precarious local monopoly. At the same time it raises another question. Since there is usually more than one shop of each kind in a large shopping centre, an "approximate long run infinite elasticity of demand" is consistent only with the assumption that the economies of scale are fairly easily exhausted. Otherwise there would be only one shop of each kind. How true is this?

The evidence is scanty, contradictory, and difficult to assess. It is quite clear that a medium-sized shop has lower costs than a very small one-man shop, if similar factors are similarly remunerated. But, of course, this is not always so. The small man who converts his parlour into a shop where he or his family serve part-time may have very low transfer costs, and be able to carry on indefinitely with low gross margins. To return, however, it is clear that where transfer earnings are similar the medium-sized shop has lower costs than the smallest shops. For example, Colin Clark's analysis[2] of the grocery trade of a number of stores controlled by a large co-operative society revealed the following situation:—

Average turnover £ per week	Costs (including interest but excluding profit) as percentage of turnover
100–200	13·21
200–300	11·51
300–400	11·13
400–500	10·50
500 upwards	10·08

[1] Differences in rent complicate the issue. Higher rents may or may not outweigh larger turnover. For department stores of equal size, rent is decisive in the United States; see E. A. Burnham, "The Department Store and its Community," *Harvard Business Review*, Vol. XVIII, p. 455. It does not seem to be so decisive in England, but the evidence is not so clear; see A. Plant and R. H. Fowler, "Costs of Retail Distribution," *Economica*, May 1939. For some theoretical discussion, see E. H. Chamberlin, loc. cit., Appendix C.

[2] C. Clark, *Conditions of Economic Progress*, p. 334.

A similar picture is suggested by Cadbury Brothers as applying to confectionery shops.[1]

It is in comparing the medium and the large shop that the evidence is inconclusive. The authors of a careful American survey[2] conclude that, apart from the high cost of the one-man business, there is "no convincing evidence of a general tendency for costs to decrease progressively as store size increases," and proceed to quote exceptions. Everything depends on the nature of the trade. The principal economy of large shopkeeping is the economy of having specialist buyers purchasing in large quantities. The more the goods can be standardised the greater is this economy. It is therefore small in the millinery business, but large in the Woolworth type of trade. The classes of shop which most multiply themselves in central shopping centres, those selling women's wear and household goods, are the classes in which standardisation tends to be least, and the advantages of scale small. The shops selling standardised goods are seldom found in great numbers even in the largest shopping centres, because it is more convenient for them to be widely distributed through the suburbs. They secure the economies of large buying through concentrating several shops under one management rather than by having a large turnover per shop; but the number of customers congregating in the centre may be sufficient to support two or three or more in any trade, each of more or less "optimum" size.

The department store fits with difficulty into the pattern of this argument. In a large shopping centre there is usually more than one. Yet the evidence is clear that there are substantial economies of scale, both in the United States[3] and in this country.[4] It is true that the American evidence shows the medium-sized department store having lowest costs, but this is because delivery and publicity expenses are higher for the largest stores, and these expenses are not relevant if we are considering merely competition between two stores in the same centre, with nearly infinite long-run cross elasticities. The large department store should be able to drive all others out of its centre simply by cutting prices. Why, also, does it not drive out the specialist shops?

[1] *Industrial Record*, 1919–39, p. 49.
[2] Twentieth Century Fund, *Does Distribution Cost Too Much?* p. 145.
[3] Cf. E. A. Burnham, "The Influence of Size of Business on Department Store Operating Results," *Harvard Business Review*, Vol. XVI, p. 211.
[4] Cf. A. Plant and R. F. Fowler, loc.

The latter is easier to answer. It must be remembered that even the largest department store is really only a collection of several small or medium-sized shops under one roof. A large department store may be able to buy more cheaply than a small one. But the shoe department of a large department store is not necessarily bigger than an independent shoe shop, and not necessarily able to buy more cheaply. Indeed, department stores are keenly conscious of the competition of the specialist shops. This is one reason why the multiple shop idea has spread over into the department store field, and why some of these multiple department stores have now adopted central buying. But the main strength of the department store is not price competition, but the fact that it offers the opportunity to buy everything under one roof, plus delivery, credit, and various amenities, and on these it concentrates its appeal. It is really doing a different class of trade from the specialist shop, and not strictly comparable.

This also yields the clue to competition between department stores themselves. The price competition is real, and governed also by the need to compete with specialist shops both at the centre and in the suburbs, which may be able to offer lower prices because they offer also less service. But because service is so important, price competition is not decisive. No two department stores have quite the same atmosphere, or give quite the same service, and the larger would not necessarily bankrupt the smaller by cutting its prices 5 per cent. Moreover, even if it could, the struggle would be long and costly. Prudence, and the small number of department stores, demand that while price competition should be real, it should be "based on costs," within the limits of what competition by specialist shops allows. In effect, the department store trade is rather special, and though it has close substitutes, is sufficiently limited for the oligopolistic phenomenon of "excess capacity" to prevail even in the shopping centre.

Moreover, in trying to analyse the existing situation, we must not treat it as if it were in "equilibrium." The department store in the 1930's was going through an awkward phase. When first it appeared, in the second half of the nineteenth century, it was a pioneer of modern methods of retailing, and its wide success was largely due to out-distancing its rivals in this respect. By the 1920's its rivals had caught up with it, and were giving it a stiff fight, and it is doubtful whether it continued to expand relatively to other forms of retail trade. It has been forced to review its policies, to decentralise internal management, to consider central buying with other stores, and to rely more and more on service. As costs of service have risen, the policy of relying on service has itself been brought into question, since some competitors, un-hampered by the high costs of free delivery, rest rooms, subsidised cafés, credit, and the rest, have pushed the price feature in their "cash and carry" policy. Most of the department stores in the United States and many in this country were losing money during the nineteen-thirties. It would be unwise to prophesy what policies they will be pursuing in the 'fifties.

8. We have thus two different types of analysis to apply to retailing, one assuming that the customers are dispersed and find a dispersal of shops convenient (with an excessive number[1] of small shops as the result), and the other assuming that the cus-tomers are concentrated in shopping centres (with the right number of shops, of optimum size). Both, of course, apply; more-over to some extent they apply to quite different classes of trade. Here the American distinction between "convenience" and "shopping" goods is useful. The former are articles purchased regularly and preferably from the nearest shop. The customer knows from daily experience just what he wants: there is no "shopping around," and the shops tend to be spread evenly over the whole area—beef, fish, cigarettes, groceries, beer, medicines and the like tend to be bought at the nearest outlet. With shopping goods, on the other hand, the customer wishes to compare prices and qualities before she makes up her mind—hats, curtains, dresses, even stockings—and the shops selling these things tend to congregate in shopping centres. The division is not watertight; some convenience goods shops of more or less optimum size are to be found in shopping centres, in competition with the suburban shops; while it is possible to find shops selling shopping goods in isolation in the suburbs, e.g. the ubiquitous draper. Department stores are in both classes of trade.

One further point is needed to complete the picture. So far we have spoken as if shops are to be found either clustered together in a central area or spread over the suburbs in lonely isolation. A little observation shows that nearly all shops are in a centre of some kind. Nevertheless the distinction between the central and the suburban shopping centres remains. The shops which are found together in the suburban shopping area tend to be shops

[1] Unless elasticity of demand is large enough to bridge the gap.

selling different classes of goods. These shops are not in close competition with each other, except in the sense in which all shops are competing for the consumers' incomes, and the fact that these different shops stand together does not invalidate the analysis. The theory of the optimum number of suburban shops becomes instead a theory of the optimum number of suburban shopping centres. Account must, however, be taken of the fact that these centres vary in size. This is due to the fact that the desirable frequency of shops varies in different trades, with the importance of overhead costs, the convenience of nearness, and the percentage of the population consuming the particular commodity. We should expect to find a large number of small centres, and smaller numbers of larger ones. Precisely where each centre is and which centres are large, are determined more by geographical considerations—the layout of streets, the junctions of main roads, the flow of traffic, and so on—than by the differential calculus, but overhead cost, density and convenience, the factors included in our calculations, are plainly not irrelevant. Ranging shopping centres in order of size, from the smallest to the largest, we should find that some suburban centres have sufficient trade to support several shops of one kind, each of optimum size, while in other trades there may be only one shop, of less than optimum size, and in others no shop at all. From the point of view of the trades in the first category this is a central shopping centre, because it is large enough to support more than one shop of optimum size, while from the point of view of the trades in the other categories it is a suburban shopping centre because it is not large enough. As the size of centres increases, so does the number of trades in which shops can be of optimum size, and to which this is a central shopping centre, until we reach the largest centres, with their department stores straining to reach the optimum.

9. We may now return to the end of section 6, where we began to take account of the effect of the existence of central shopping centres on shops in the suburbs. The first effect is a tendency for shops to be both smaller and at greater distances than they would be from each other, because the density of buying population in the suburbs is reduced. On the other hand, suburban shopkeepers, having to face the competition of central shopping areas, are less likely to try to exploit local monopoly positions, and this increase in competitiveness is a factor on the side of lower prices and fewer and larger shops. The extent of price competition, however,

varies. In price-maintained convenience goods trades—and nearly all such trades are price-maintained—the suburban shop-keeper faces only competition in service, which, at a distance, may not be very effective. In such trades it is certain that there will be too many shops. In the shopping goods trades the position is different; the suburban shops are faced with both price and service competition from shops of optimum size at the centre, and are compelled to keep their prices as low as is consistent with the fact that they themselves cannot attain to optimum size. (This is one of the reasons why price maintenance is unlikely to spread over into such trades.)

10. We may conclude by summarising:—

(a) Suburban shops should be of less than optimum size; if there is free entry into retailing they will be smaller and more numerous than they should be, unless elasticity of demand is large enough to bridge the gap; and if there is price maintenance they will be still smaller and more numerous, with perhaps too much service.

(b) Free delivery and other discriminatory services tend to bring shops nearer the ideal size and number.

(c) In central shopping centres shops will be of optimum size, and shops selling shopping goods will tend to cluster together here; department stores are an exception in that they are probably too numerous and too small.

II

COMPETITION IN SERVICE

1. Retailing is not a homogeneous "commodity"; it varies widely in quality, and correspondingly in cost. We must now examine the contention that the effect of competition is an excess of the more expensive forms, as well as the reverse contention, that competition causes the quality of the service to deteriorate.

It is useful to begin by distinguishing the features which make for expense. One is the very existence of service. "Help yourself" shops exist in the United States, and show the lowest margins of all. Then there is the speed with which service is effected—how long the customer has to wait before an assistant attends to him. Speedy service is particularly costly because the flow of customers into the shop is irregular. If the shop tried to keep enough assistants to be able to deal with the largest number of customers ever likely

COMPETITION IN RETAIL TRADE

to be in the shop, most of these would be idle for much of the time, sales per assistant low and operating costs high. In retailing as in transport, costs would be much reduced if customers could distribute themselves evenly throughout the day and (though this is not so important) throughout the year. Next comes the quality of the assistants. In some trades the customer relies on the shop-keeper for information on the comparative qualities of the merchandise, and shop assistants have to be specialists trained in its qualities and uses. This means not only a more expensive kind of assistant, but also a smaller average number of customers per assistant than in, for example, the Woolworth type of trade. Another important service is performed when the shop offers the customer a wide choice of styles, colours, sizes or makes from which to suit his requirements. Some shops, especially depart-ment stores, add to this the right to return the purchase if on going home the customer changes her mind—American depart-ment stores report that one day's sales in eight are returned[1] —and find this a heavy burden. Lifts, escalators, rest rooms, credit, free delivery, information—the list becomes too long for elaboration.

Account must also be taken of forms of retailing which do not involve the customer in going to the shop. Orders by telephone or by mail are convenient if the customer knows just what he wants, and this form of business has low operating costs. Or the shop may go to the customer, in the form of the travelling van or the door-to-door salesman. Here operating costs are usually high.

2. In order to arrive at the conclusion that competition leads to an excess of the more expensive forms of retailing, in sub-stitution for the less expensive, it is necessary to establish one of two propositions—either that customers get what they want, but should not be allowed to get it; or that they get what they do not want, through market imperfection. The first proposition has its adherents; they admit that the customer prefers good service even when there is a real choice open to him of less expensive forms, but they contend that this is a luxury he should not be allowed. In wartime we have all accepted this view in the United Kingdom, in order to release resources for other purposes. In peacetime too, "productive" output would be greater if "dis-tributive" activity were curtailed, and in a planned economy a

[1] Twentieth Century Fund, op. cit., p. 308.

planning authority which attached little value to convenience in shopping relatively to increased outputs of other utilities would undoubtedly take steps to restrict the more expensive forms of retailing. In this country, however, where women exercise the vote, such restrictions are unlikely. To a busy woman—and with the decline of domestic service and the increased entry of women into jobs and professions nearly all women will be busy women— good shopping facilities are essential; if she can get served without waiting, see at once a wide range from which to choose, and obtain delivery, she can get back rapidly to her duties; to reduce such facilities would mean that the public spent more time in shopping, and some of what was gained in distribution costs would be lost in other ways.

It is more important to examine the proposition that some who would prefer less service and lower prices are deprived of it. This depends on market imperfection. In a large shopping centre where all kinds of shops are competing it is highly unlikely. There are shops with much service and high prices, and shops with less service and lower prices, and the customers are free to sort themselves out. In 1931 one of America's leading authorities on retailing[1] wrote:—

"To judge from what is happening in the department store field and from what is happening in the chain store field, it is a fair generalisation that types of distributive enterprise tend to develop through three stages. They start off very largely on a price basis—as chain stores did, for instance they catch the attention of the consumer by distributing merchandise at low prices because of a low overhead. That is the first stage. The next stage is the 'trading up' of the quality of the merchandise handled. We can see chain stores going through that stage to-day. After they have traded up the quality of the merchandise handled, and some of the price advantage has been lost in the process, distributive enterprises develop into a third stage, characterised by competition in services of all kinds, for instance in allowing customers to return merchandise; by high costs of doing business; by largely competitive advertising; and by an increase in the ratio of the fixed investment to the total investment. Department stores to-day are in that stage."

[1] M. P. McNair, "Trends in Large Scale Retailing," *Harvard Business Review*, Vol. X, p. 39.

This would seem to support the view that the public inevitably prefers better services to low prices, but events have not justified this conclusion. The department stores, having reached the third stage, have found themselves losing so much to cheaper rivals (including the "super-market," which was just making its appearance when the passage was written) that they have greatly extended their "bargain basements," and some of them are beginning to urge on the fraternity that delivery and similar services should be charged for separately, so that the stores can retain some of the custom they have been losing to cheaper rivals. The tendency to higher costs, if it exists, is only like an escalator in the sense that as fast as some move up others come in at the bottom; the better simile would be a cycle, since the fourth stage brings lower costs than the third. The fact that the public is free to choose between the cheaper and the more expensive acts as a check preventing too much service from being offered.

The practice of "price lining" may seem to support the opposite view. If prices tend to stick around certain figures, e.g. the elevenpence three-farthingses, increased efficiency would seem to lead not to lower prices but to better quality at the same price. This, however, is an illusion, since this better quality now sold cheaply was formerly sold at some higher price level. Price lining prevents prices from being continuously variable, but it does not prevent them from falling.

However, we cannot apply the same analysis to shops situated not in central but in local markets. There the element of local monopoly means that the customer has not an effective choice between several shops offering different degrees of service. Here there may well be too much service, especially in price-maintained trades, in the sense that some customers are getting more than they want. In non-price-maintained trades the competitive incentive is not so much to offer service as such, if the shop is able to offer different customers different degrees of service, as to offer types of service which involve price discrimination in favour of marginal customers, and which tend therefore to bring the shop nearer to the ideal size. Is this desirable, or does it mean that there is too much service? There are two sides to the argument. Clearly there is too much service in the sense that the marginal customers are getting more than they pay for: they are being subsidised. On the other hand, since the shop will have more customers, shops will be larger, fewer in number, and less costly. It is the old argument for price discrimination in new form.

If the services offered are real, and performed at minimum cost, we can say that there will not be too much service even in imperfect competition, provided that the imperfection is not due to any significant extent to "irrational" elements. The three services which most merit analysis in this light are information, a range of styles, and delivery.

3. Information is a real service. We are all conscious of the wastes involved in competitive advertising, and tend to dismiss all publicity expenditure as wasteful. That it is not necessarily so has long been emphasised in economic literature.[1] For a market to be perfect all the buyers and all the sellers must know what is available and at what prices. Publicity expenditure which serves this purpose is really useful. Advertising is wasteful only when it is unnecessary because buyers and sellers already know the facts, or when it is false or misleading. Now, while much advertising by manufacturers is wasteful for these reasons, this is not usually the case with retailers' advertisements. Actually, only a very small proportion of retailers think it worth while to advertise, this itself being a tribute to the fact that the retail market is not as imperfect as some writers have suggested. And perusal of the advertisements published by retailers will show that while the element of reputation building is not absent, they tend to concentrate on straightforward information about particular lines which are on offer. It seems therefore legitimate to conclude that in retailing such publicity expenditure as there is performs for the most part a valuable service.

We cannot, however, dismiss manufacturers' advertisements as irrelevant to competition in retailing, for they are not. Since there is competition, every retailer is subject to pressures requiring him to stock as wide a range as his customers are likely to want to choose from, and this is indeed a factor on which manufacturers strongly rely in spending money an advertisements. This, therefore, brings us straight to the second problem, the range of goods retailers carry.

4. If in each commodity demand concentrated on one or two styles, economies of scale could be exploited, and prices would be lower. This is the basic case for the "utility" scheme in wartime

[1] E.g. D. Braithwaite, "The Economic Effects of Advertising," *Economic Journal*, March 1928.

England. The first question is therefore why the market itself does not provide for getting these economies. To some extent it does. If a retailer finds that by concentrating all his efforts on a single style he can buy and sell more cheaply, he has an incentive to do so. The Woolworth type of business, which is one of the most successful forms of retailing, is based on this principle; the multiple shops, the department stores, and many independents also work on this basis to a larger extent than is generally recognised by those who advocate that the "utility" scheme should be made permanent. Broadly speaking, standardisation is the basis of large-scale retailing, and one of the reasons why in so many lines of production the retailer dominates the manufacturer.[1] In small-scale retailing, the retailer is not able to give large orders in standard designs, but relies rather on the wholesaler to do this. The wholesaler is to the small retailer as the centralised buying department is to the multiple shop, and if wholesalers were as efficient as the buyers of large-scale retailing, the whole pattern of retailing would be different. When Mr. Schumacher suggests virtually a state monopoly of wholesaling as the simplest way to control both production and distribution,[2] he certainly puts his finger on the central weakness in the distributive chain (whatever the merits of the particular proposal). More efficient wholesaling would deprive the larger retailers of their principal advantage over the small, and would promote greater standardisation of manufactures.

But, whatever the desire of large retail buyers or wholesalers to standardise, two other forces act as a check. One is the creation of "consumer insistence" by manufacturers' advertisements. The case made for such advertising is varied. (a) Some useful commodities, e.g. the typewriter, would never have reached the public as quickly without it. This is undoubtedly true; some advertising performs the useful function of information. But this does not apply to all the £80,000,000 to £100,000,000 a year spent on advertising in this country.[3] (b) Advertising frequently leads not to an increase but to a reduction in the number of styles, and to savings in production cost, by persuading the public

[1] Nearly all the important groups of multiple shops in this country are manufacturer chains, in contradistinction to the United States.
[2] E. F. Schumacher, "An Essay on State Control," *Agenda*, February 1944.
[3] This is the estimate made by F. P. Bishop, *The Economics of Advertising*, Ch. III.

to concentrate most of its purchases on one or two well-advertised brands. This also is true. But the opposite is also frequently true; and if from the £100,000,000 we must subtract something for the cases where economies of scale are secured, if we are to have the true cost of advertising, we must also add something for the cases where consumer insistence hinders standardisation. Mr. Bishop also advances two other ingenious arguments. (c) Advertising makes people want things. they cannot afford; it therefore increases the propensity to consume and consequently increases employment. The argument might be impressive if there were not less costly ways of maintaining employment, but as there are, economists cannot be expected to take the argument seriously. (d) The Press is always subsidised; where proprietors cannot get revenue from advertisers they sell themselves to political parties or the Government, and in the long run subsidy by advertisement is far more healthy for the public. This may be true. But there are alternatives. If the Government decided to prohibit advertising in the Press, and if the Press must be subsidised, let the Government undertake to pay a subsidy varying only with circulation; e.g. to pay newspaper proprietors 1d. for each copy sold, on the understanding that there shall be no advertisements. Provided the subsidy were open to all on these terms, the Press would remain independent and free to criticise. It would in fact be much freer than it is to-day, when the political and other views of large advertisers have to be borne in mind.

Some reformers are content to try to control the impact of advertising. There are some who advocate strict legal controls, penalising misrepresentation, as the Federal Trade Commission seeks to do in the United States.[1] Others hope that in this country, as in the United States, independent testing agencies will grow up, private- or State-maintained, to inform the consumer of the true merits of different brands. Or even that the Press will allow manufacturers to speak plainly in their advertisements about the inferiority of their rivals' products.[2] To the present writer none of this seems sufficiently fundamental. What is of value in the case for manufacturers' advertisement is that it supplies information, and that it sometimes concentrates demand on a few styles. But

[1] For a discussion of American attitudes and practices, see M. G. Reid, *Consumers and the Market*, Part VI.
[2] Cf. the discussion by A. Plant, "The Distribution of Proprietary Articles," in *Some Modern Business Problems*, ed. Plant.

both these services could be supplied equally by retailers, at less cost, and more impartially, especially if greater steps, voluntary or compulsory, were taken to promote standardisation, and more so still if something like Chamberlin's advocacy of trade mark infringement proved practicable.[1] It should not be on the manufacturer's strident claims that the public has to rely for information. The retailer, usually a better judge of merchandise than the consumer, is better able to decide which brand is worth buying in large quantities, and pushing. In the view of the present writer, while branding should be retained to facilitate identification, manufacturers should be allowed to advertise only in trade journals for circulation amongst wholesalers and retailers, and not in the ordinary Press. In this country we have already banned advertisement from the wireless, will, it is to be hoped, ban it from the sky, and are always talking about banning it from the hoardings. To ban it from the ordinary Press would not be as revolutionary as it sounds, and would also greatly increase the perfection of the market, and reduce waste.

There remains, however, a further check on retailers which prevents them from carrying as small a range of styles as they might otherwise desire. It is the desire of their customers to be able to choose from as wide a range as possible, and indeed, in some cases, notably women's wear, the desire to have something different from what other people will have. In some cases, in a large shopping centre, this does not matter. If there are enough people who prefer cheapness and standardisation to variety, some retailers will be able to concentrate on mass lines, and to secure for such consumers all the economies of scale. But in other trades it may remain the case that if all customers were compelled to accept the standard brand, costs would be lower than they could be without such compulsion. Should such compulsion be exercised? This is clearly a question for the philosopher rather than for the economist.

5. We come, thirdly, to delivery costs. That the several vans of different shops should be delivering in the same road has long seemed a conspicuous source of waste. The waste, however, such as it is, consists not in the fact of delivery, but in the inefficiency with which delivery is organised. If shopkeepers would use, not their own delivery vans but the services offered by public transport contractors, costs would be reduced, as each contractor could

[1] Cp. cit., Appendix E.

deliver on behalf of several different shops. Competition between the shops would not be affected by this any more than competition between manufacturers is affected by common use of the railway system or the post office. That they do not use public transport facilities is due principally to the fact that the convenience of delivering for oneself (plus the slight advertisement value of having one's own vans) outweighs what would be saved. This applies equally to pooled delivery services, such as have been enforced in wartime. Moreover, there is reason to believe that the extent of possible savings is grossly exaggerated. The case most quoted in England is milk delivery. Yet an independent investigator, who made a careful survey in Battersea, concluded[1]:—

"To limit the number of distributors to a maximum of four in any road would cause such a small increase in the sales of these four as to have an almost negligible effect upon costs. To limit the number to two in this area would increase the sales of the two largest distributors by 66 per cent, but one is not convinced that even to limit it to one distributor would materially reduce the large distributor's costs. With the largest distributor only a small portion of the roundsman's time is taken in covering the actual length of road; most is taken in going from door to door, in bringing the customer to the door and engaging her in conversation. In one respect only does it seem probable that giving a particular area completely to one milkman would materially reduce costs, and that is in preventing people from buying from two or more distributors. In this area 11 per cent of the families bought from two or more distributors; in Oxford, Dr. Murray found nearly 15 per cent dealt with two dairymen. This seems a complete waste, and probably its abolition would reduce distributive costs by 10 per cent, say at least 1d. per gallon.

The principal cause of waste in milk distribution, of course, is the fact that the authorities have maintained the minimum retail price at a level allowing a margin so grossly in excess of the costs of large and efficient distributors that an altogether excessive number of firms is able to exist, and also an excessive amount of service.[2]

[1] H. S. Booker, "A Survey of Milk Distribution," *Economica*, February 1939.
[2] The facts are given in two official papers: *Report by the Food Council to the President of the Board of Trade on Costs and Profits of Retail Milk Distribution in Great Britain*, 1937, and *Report of a Committee appointed to examine Costs of Milk Distribution*, 1940.

6. Finally we must consider the proposition that competition causes service to deteriorate. The shopkeeper, it is said, pressed by competition, and unable to make both ends meet, is driven to reduce the quality of the product and the service, and to misrepresentation and fraud.

To say that the quality will deteriorate is only another way of saying that the price will rise in competition, and we have already examined the conditions in which this is possible. In a really competitive market a shopkeeper may offer less value for the same money, but this will usually be on his way out. If consumers are unable at the time of making a purchase to distinguish between good and bad quality, a retailer may pass off bad as good, but the consumer will discover the difference on using the article, and retailers who do this will lose goodwill and disappear. It remains possible that there are articles whose quality the consumer cannot distinguish even in the course of use, and which he buys relying solely on the retailer's advice, or on high price as a guarantee of quality. Much is made of this by some writers, quoting quality tests which show low correlation between quality and price. The range of articles to which this applies cannot be very great, and would be smaller still if some teaching on how to use the market were supplied to the consumer through the Press, the wireless, films, women's institutes, guilds, unions, and other media for adult education.

That competition may stimulate fraud cannot be questioned. In some countries the primitive view prevails that every act of sale is a battle of wits, and even the strictest laws prohibiting adulteration or controlling weights and measures or the like cannot entirely outlaw sharp practice. Honesty is the best policy only where shopkeepers are competing in honesty; not where they are competing in dishonesty. Fortunately in this country the competitive forces work in the right direction. Especially is this so where the shopkeeper depends on the regular support of a loyal clientele, and cannot afford to lose their goodwill. It is less so where the customer will buy from any seller infrequently— perhaps only once—as in buying durable goods or buying in the course of a journey. Here the shopkeeper may be tempted to follow too literally the Biblical injunction to take in the stranger. If he does this consistently he will probably sooner or later get a bad name and disappear; but he may get away with it, if done infrequently, or may be replaced merely by someone else who follows the same policy. The best safeguard for the public is to learn to shop around making enquiries before committing oneself to the purchase of expensive durable goods.

7. We may now summarise the conclusions of this section as follows:—

(a) In large shopping centres it is unlikely that more service is provided than is wanted; competition between different forms of retailing tends to prevent such waste.

(b) In smaller suburban centres some customers may receive some service which they would rather not have; others, through price discrimination, receive more service than they are willing to pay for, but the effect of this is to make shops nearer ideal size.

(c) All forms of retailing might have lower costs but for manufacturers' advertisements to the public, and but for the public's desire for variety of styles. How far these should be controlled, however, raises issues independent of the degree of competition in retailing.

(d) Service may deteriorate as a result of competition, but this is not likely in this country.

III

UNFAIR COMPETITION

1. In this section we are concerned with arguments that certain forms of competition are unfair and distort the distributive process. The practices in question are (a) claiming the status of a retailer without fulfilling all the functions; (b) "poaching" in one trade by retailers in another (e.g. grocers selling patent medicines); (c) direct sales to the public at "wholesale" prices; (d) "special" prices to large traders; (e) gift coupons and trading stamps; and (f) sales to co-operative societies.

2. We can begin with two points common to all these problems. The first is that the retailer's criterion of what is fair is not the economist's. The retailer characterises as unfair almost anything which upsets his expectations, especially if it does so by diverting trade to a different form of retailing. The economist cannot condemn a practice solely on these grounds.

Secondly, underlying most of these cases is the belief that distortion of the "normal" channels of distribution raises costs. Coupon trading is a good example of this. If chocolate manufacturers give away cameras in redemption of coupons, the retailers of cameras claim that this reduces the sales of cameras through existing outlets, and therefore increases costs. All the forms of "unfair competition" listed above would be attacked on this ground, among others.

For this line of argument to be valid, four propositions must be established. First, that the new form of retailing does diminish the business done by the old. Secondly, that when the business done by the old diminishes, the effect is an increase in its costs, i.e. that the number of shops does not diminish *pari passu*, the remaining shops having the same average turnover as before. Thirdly, that the costs of the new form exceed the marginal costs of the old. And fourthly, that the difference in costs is not justified to the consumer by difference in service or other convenience.

It is not always accepted that the new form of retailing diminishes the business done by the old. For example, some supporters of gift coupons claim that the persons who get cameras through this medium would for the most part not be willing to buy cameras, and that having got the cameras they buy films from photographic dealers and have them developed, so that the trade of the ordinary dealer is not reduced but increased. It is always possible in some cases that the extension of a new cheap form of retailing may so expand demand that even the older and more expensive forms of retailing also benefit (just as publication in the "Penguin" series sometimes increases sales of the expensive edition of a book), but there must also be many cases in which the net effect is that the turnover of the older forms is reduced.

If this is the case, the effect will be different in large shopping centres and in small. The large shopping centre being defined, for any given commodity, as one where the number of customers is large enough to support several shops each of optimum size, the effect will be simply that one or more of these shops is put out of business, the others keeping the same size, costs and prices. In the smaller centres, however, the effect is different. Unless the new form replaces the old form altogether, its effect is to detach some customers lying within the area of each shop. This is a reduction in the density of the buying population, which, as we have already seen, results in smaller shops and higher costs.

When this is the case, some customers are benefiting from the new form of competition at the expense of others who pay higher prices. If it were possible for all customers to transfer to the new form, the public would not be harmed by this. For example, if it could be shown that the effect of the spread of co-operatives was not simply to bankrupt some private traders, but rather to raise the prices paid by non-co-operators, no economist would justify restrictions on co-operatives on this ground, since it is open to all customers to join co-operatives. But the case is different with coupon trading; we cannot advise all persons who want cameras to get them through eating chocolates. Where the cheaper form of distribution is not open to all, the problem is more difficult.

The key to the solution is total costs. If the sum of the costs of the total sales under new and old systems is less than it would cost to distribute the same output through the old system exclusively, the new form is justified. This will be the case so long as the costs (prime plus fixed) of the new form of retailing are less than the marginal costs of the old. But the new form will not be justified even if its average cost (and price) is less than the average cost (and price) of the old if it is not also less than the marginal cost of the old. In these conditions a case can be made for prohibiting the new form of retailing. The problem arises only because some retailers who have falling average costs cannot discriminate in favour of the type of customer to whom the new form of retailing makes its restricted appeal. If they could discriminate they could prevent the new form from establishing itself by quoting prices, based on marginal cost, less than the new form could support. As they cannot discriminate, the new form emerges, and social costs are increased.

To complete the argument, it must be shown that the customers who would patronise the new form would gain only to the extent of the lower price; that there is no special convenience or service attached to the new form, such as would justify higher social costs; in a word, that the two forms of retailing are nearly perfect substitutes. Thus the suburban shopkeeper cannot argue that the cheap shops in the centre should be closed even if he could show that their average costs exceed his marginal costs, for shopping in the suburbs is not an exact substitute for shopping in the centre, and many people who live in the suburbs would find it more convenient to shop in the centre even if prices were the same. Nor, to turn the argument round, can the cheaper forms of retailing apply a similar argument for eliminating the more expensive; the two are not exact substitutes. For the argument to be applicable it must be shown that the price is the only practical difference from the consumer's point of view.

It seems a revolutionary conclusion that costs can sometimes be reduced by eliminating the "cheaper" forms of retailing, but as we shall see, the practical significance of the conclusion is very limited. Let us now take each form of "unfair" competition in turn.

3. A number of retail trade associations in this country have agreed with manufacturers or wholesalers that a person should not receive retailer's discounts on his purchases unless he has or is prepared to have a regular shop, open at the usual hours, carrying certain minimum stocks, and perhaps offering after-sales or other usual services. This "fair trading" policy, as it is called, is found, for example, in the bookselling, photographic and motor car trades.[1] This sort of policy is aimed partly at the small part-time retailer, who keeps a parlour shop, partly at "poaching" in one trade by members of another, and partly at direct sales to the public at wholesale prices. It thus covers the first three cases on our list.

It is most unlikely that this restriction could be justified on the ground that the average costs of those excluded exceed the marginal costs of those that remain. The real costs of the man with the parlour shop are low, because his transfer costs and rent are low. So also are the costs of the "poacher," who enters the extra trade usually because he has already under-utilised premises and staff for his own trade. From the point of view of real costs, one can say broadly that the more "poaching" there is the better, since this gives the average shop in each district a larger total trade and lower costs (the limit to "poaching" is set by the advantages of specialisation). And as for sales direct to the public at wholesale prices, this is the case least likely to fit the argument, since the consumer's cost of retailing to himself is zero (though he may have a heavier transport cost). The "fair trading" policy cannot therefore be justified on the ground that sales through these channels are uneconomic.

Neither is the justification usually attempted on these lines. First, in some trades the retailer says, in effect, "To do my

[1] The fullest survey of the facts about each of the principal retail trades is to be found in a series of articles published in the *Manchester Guardian Commercial Weekly* in the second half of 1938 and the first half of 1939. For books and motor cars the relevant dates are June 24, 1938, and October 28, 1938.

K

business properly I must carry a wide range of models, to offer the
public a good choice; it is unfair that I should lose trade to someone
who does not do the same." It is not unfair that some shops should
stock less wide ranges than others; those customers who wish to
be able to consult a wide range are free to do so at the more
expensive shops, while others may chose the cheaper. But the
argument is more subtle. The retailer with the wide range argues
that other retailers benefit from his policy; sales in the other
shops are larger because there are shops displaying a wide range;
in effect the retailer with the wide range is bearing part of the
"information" costs of the whole trade. The argument is un-
impressive; no retailer is compelled to act in this philanthropic
way. If he really thinks that it is possible to thrive off other
people's stock carrying, there is nothing to stop him from doing
so. This, however, brings us to the second argument. Manufacturers frequently support the fair trading policy because they
think that it is in the interest of the trade as a whole that retailers
should carry a wide range of stocks; it has advertising value, and
causes total sales to be greater. In discriminating against retailers
who do not carry this range they are in effect paying a subsidy
to others for advertising. The desirability of this rests therefore on
the desirability of advertising, and in particular of advertising
simply to divert demand from other commodities to the advertised.
This can hardly be justified as "information." The public knows
of the existence of the particular class of merchandise, and
multiplication of the varieties within the class in order specially
to catch its eye deserves no special protection. The third argument
is more weighty. It is that in certain trades the retailer should
have special qualifications, e.g. that in the photographic trade the
public would be badly served by retailers who gave bad advice
on the respective merits of cameras, or bad after-sales service.
Where the commodity is purchased frequently, the public needs
no such certificate of qualification; the buyer soon finds out for
himself whether his grocer is to be trusted. But where the service
is infrequent, some certificate would be useful; e.g. how is the
householder to know whether the radio dealer round the corner
can really mend a silent wireless set without at the same time
doing irremediable and temporarily concealed damage inside?
There is something to be said for requiring retailers in certain
durable goods trades to pass some test of competence, particularly
in the photographic trade, radios, and garages, as is already done

for chemists; or at least for an optional test, enabling the public to distinguish between certified and uncertified. But it is a fundamental principle that such tests must be conducted independently, and not by interested parties, such as manufacturers or a retail trade association.

Lastly, sales to the public at "wholesale" prices are opposed on the ground that it is unfair that the retailer should face such competition from the people who sell to him. This is indeed a common complaint, especially in the drapery, sports goods, cycle, meat, jewellery and outfitting trades,[1] and includes protests against sales to members of clubs at special prices. The saying that "only saps pay retail prices" indicates how common is the practice. A manufacturer (or wholesaler) may adopt it in one of two circumstances. It may be that he is able to distribute to the consumer at a cost less than the margin the retailer claims. If the retailer's margin barely covers the retailer's costs, this means that the manufacturer is able to distribute more cheaply by direct methods of sale, and there is no case for preventing him from doing this. But it may be that the margin exceeds retailers' costs, and that the efficient retailers are prevented from reducing their prices by a resale price maintenance scheme. It would certainly be unfair of manufacturers to undersell retailers who are compelled to maintain prices, but the problem this raises is whether prices should be maintained in this way, and this is reserved for the final part of this paper.

Alternatively, the manufacturer may be discriminating, and earning a higher profit on his sales to retailers than on his sales to the public. This is unlikely to be profitable if it results in sales to the public expanding at the expense of sales to retailers—and if it does not the retailer has no ground for complaint, because the manufacturer is then substituting less for more profitable sales, unless the expansion of direct sales is much greater than the decline of sales through retailers.

A similar problem arises in connection with the allegation that large retailers flourish as a result of obtaining special prices. This problem has arisen much more acutely in the United States than

---

[1] See the relevant articles in the *Manchester Guardian Commercial Weekly* of August 12, 1938, September 16, 1938, September 23, 1938, November 11, 1938, November 18, 1938, and December 2, 1938. For an American discussion see G. B. Tallman, "When Customers buy at Wholesale," *Harvard Business Review*, Vol. XVII, p. 339.

it has in this country, where the multiple shops are much less aggressively competitive than their American counterparts. The rôle of the chain in the American distributive set-up is played in this country in a different way by the co-operative movement. Multiple, chain and co-operative owe a great part of their success to buying more cheaply than the independent shop. That there are real economies reflected in the lower prices they pay is not open to question; the large retailing organisations relieve the manufacturer of many costs he would incur if selling to small shops, and they perform the wholesaling functions for themselves more cheaply and efficiently than the wholesale firms do for the small independent shop. Nevertheless it is possible that they also get discriminatory prices, based on their great bargaining power. In the United States, where the problem has been widely debated and officially investigated, the evidence is not conclusive.[1] Three reactions may be noted. The first is the "classification" of customers in trade categories. Here, trade associations bring pressure to bear on manufacturers to base their discounts on the trade status of the buyer rather than on quantity bought, so that the price charged for any given quantity will be different according to whether the buyer is a consumer, a retailer, or a wholesaler. This policy is clearly uneconomic from the public point of view, since it hampers the development of efficient large-scale retailing, and tends to ossify the structure of distribution and to preserve intermediaries beyond the extent justified by the services they perform. The second possible reaction is legislation against price discrimination; in the United States the Robinson-Patman Act is intended specially to protect the small shopkeeper against discrimination. The object of such legislation is laudable; some discrimination between consumers can be defended, where average costs are falling, if it brings output nearer the ideal (especially if the discrimination is in favour of the lower income groups), but discrimination between retailers and consumers or between different classes of intermediaries is unfair in itself, as well as likely to cause an uneconomic distortion of the distributive structure. To prevent it by legislation is nevertheless a formidable task. Rather more perhaps may be hoped from the third reaction. This is for retailers to co-operate in buying, so as to secure the full economies of scale. The co-operative retail buying movement has spread very rapidly

---

[1] For a summary of the discussion, see Twentieth Century Fund, op. cit., p. 83.

in the United States, where it has saved the small shopkeeper, but has made little progress in the United Kingdom, where small retailers prefer the protection of "classification" and price maintenance. Co-operative buying is undoubtedly the most desirable reaction from the public point of view.

4. Retailers object to the distribution of goods through gift coupons and trading stamp schemes because it interferes with their trade. No case can be made out on the basis of real costs. The real costs of handling the goods distributed in this way seem to be rather low, as the work is done on a large scale; on the whole, the customer gets good value for his money. More interesting is the argument that the use of coupons and trading stamps increases market imperfection; customers are tied to particular commodities by coupons, or to particular retailers by trading stamps, and may have their attention diverted from the quality of the goods they are buying, or the prices charged, by the illusion of "getting something for nothing." Some countries have indeed prohibited or restricted coupon trading, usually in order to protect retailers, but the Board of Trade Committee which investigated the practice in 1933[1] concluded that the public suffers no harm, and no new evidence or arguments have since emerged to overthrow this conclusion. Coupon trading, however, is just an adjunct to non-price competition between manufacturers and to manufacturers' advertisements; and the trading stamp is primarily the product of resale price maintenance. If these sources of market imperfection were removed most of this form of trading would disappear.

5. The view that the consumers' co-operative movement is in some sense unfair still seems to persist in some quarters in this country, though recent events suggest that it does not turn many votes! To discuss the argument that the principle of co-operative trading is itself unfair would strain the reader's patience. Only special points deserve mention. One is the suggestion that the co-operative surplus is to some extent due to special prices secured from manufacturers by bargaining power. There is no evidence of this. The exhaustive enquiry published in 1938[2] showed that the surplus arises out of the real economies of co-operative trading, especially lower publicity, rent and interest costs, but above all wholesaling economies. A second point is the insistence of some

---

[1] *Report of the Committee on Gift Coupons and Trading Stamps*, Cmd. 4385 of 1933.

[2] A. M. Carr-Saunders, P. Sargant Florence, and R. Peers, *Consumers' Co-operation in Great Britain*, esp. Chs. XXII and XXIII.

retail trade associations that where resale prices are maintained it would be unfair to allow co-operatives to pay dividends on purchases of these goods, since the dividend would represent a form of undercutting for which private traders would be penalised. There is some substance in the argument, but its final validity depends on the case for price maintenance, which we shall discuss in the last part of this paper. Finally, it is argued that it is unfair that co-operative dividends are not subject to taxation. The literature on the point is large. The opinion of the present writer is that the co-operative surplus is not comparable with the private trader's profit. That profit contains two elements, remuneration for his labour, and interest on his capital. The comparable items in co-operative trading are the salary paid to managers and the interest paid on shares; the surplus partakes of neither of these elements, but is rather a form of voluntary saving. This view is not, however, accepted universally by economists.[1]

6. We may therefore conclude as to unfair competition that the only valid and significant case is that against price discrimination between classes of buyers, in accordance with trade status; price differentiation should be based rather on the cost of handling quantities.

IV

LIMITATIONS ON COMPETITION

1. To many traders what is unfair is not just certain forms of competition, but the very fact of competition itself, whether it be competition in price, service competition, or the entry of new firms into a trade. Several retail trade associations operate schemes to enforce resale price maintenance, and many would like to imitate the newsagents in enforcing a distance limit.

2. It is not surprising that most retailers of convenience goods, operating as they must on a small scale in local markets, favour price maintenance. It seems to offer them protection from the large shops, of optimum size, in the large centres, who, correspondingly, are on the whole against price maintenance. The protection is illusory. In price maintenance the margin is set normally high enough to cover the costs of most retailers in the trade, and, if competition does not whittle profits away in more costly service,

---

[1] For discussion, see D. H. Macgreggor, "The Taxation of Co-operative Dividend," *Economic Journal*, March 1933, and C. R. Fay, "Co-operators and the State," ibid., September 1933.

either more retailers are attracted or "poaching" spreads; the number of outlets increases, and turnover per outlet falls; costs per unit of sales rise; pressure is applied for a still higher margin; this attracts still more outlets; and the cycle continues. From the point of view of the retailer, even the highest margin will barely cover his costs, because the number of outlets, and turnover per outlet, will be adjusted to whatever the margin may be. So long, therefore, as there is free entry into a trade, directly or by "poaching," price maintenance is no protection from competition; it is merely a costly and wasteful burden on the public. The drug trade is the stock example of what happens. Before price maintenance was adopted, the number of outlets for patent medicines more or less equalled the number of chemists; to-day, because of the attractive margins, other shops have taken up patent medicines, and outnumber the chemists in this trade by ten to one. Similarly in the tobacco trade there are 23 "poachers" to every one tobacconist, and in the confectionery trade five "poachers" to every "legitimate" confectioner. The chemists have now been driven to bringing organised pressure to bear on manufacturers to restrict the sale of patent medicines to qualified chemists.

Surprise has been expressed that manufacturers should support price maintenance, instead of wishing their goods to be retailed as cheaply as possible. Fear of the repercussions of the "loss leader" has some significance, but only in relation to the more fundamental explanation. The fact is that in many classes of trade sales depend more on there being many outlets than on low prices. This is the reason why the State has for centuries restricted the number of public-houses, and it applies with equal force to confectionery, newspapers, books or cigarettes. Moreover, within any of these classes of trade, it may be of greater advantage to a manufacturer to have his brand available in every shop, than to have it available at a low price. These advertising considerations make manufacturers willing to fix margins high enough to encourage even the least efficient and smallest retailers to stock the brand, and to take the elaborate steps necessary to avoid a differentially low price level or loss leaders in the large central markets which would draw trade from the smaller shops and discourage them from stocking the brand.[1] For shopping goods, which are sold mostly in

[1] In a few cases of price maintenance the manufacturer of a widely advertised brand puts a standard price on the article which allows the retailer only a very small margin. Here the manufacturer is anxious that it be sold as

large shopping centres where sales depend on keen prices rather than on wide stocking, resale prices are never likely to be fixed.

From the public's point of view resale price maintenance is doubly condemned (*a*) because it causes the number of shops and the amount of service to be excessive and prices to be too high; and (*b*) because manufacturers promote it for advertising reasons. And the fact that it does not really in the long run shelter the shopkeeper from competition simply removes any ground for sympathy, and makes the system all the more absurd. It is hardly necessary to consider two arguments which are sometimes advanced; that the public gains from price maintenance because the system tends to enforce a maximum price as well as a minimum, so that the customer cannot be defrauded; or that the public would not have "confidence" in a commodity found selling in different shops at different prices. If it is maximum prices that benefit the public, then fix not minimum but maximum prices; and what happens to public confidence in that wide range of commodities whose retail prices are not fixed?

The case against price maintenance is beyond doubt. It is one of the major sources of waste in distribution, and the public would benefit greatly if it and the boycotts, stop lists, discrimination against co-operative societies, and other paraphernalia by which the system is enforced were made illegal.

3. The licensing of shops, however, raises more difficult problems. We have seen that, even if prices are not maintained, the number of suburban shops may be excessive. A prima facie case for restriction is therefore established.

Any such proposal, however, has to meet a formidable array of objections. First, many people are anxious to maintain an open door in retailing as a refuge for the small man from "wage slavery" into "independence." In many quarters the small trader is regarded as the pillar of society, a view which cannot always survive closer examination of his outlook and prejudices. But, whatever the merits of the small trader, it is certainly not kind to encourage large numbers of small men to enter into retailing. By and large,

cheaply as possible; he hopes that his advertising will compel most retailers to stock it, and knows that more would stock it if the margin were wider, but nevertheless prefers a lower price to wider stocking. His standard price is really a *maximum* price. This is quite a different case from the normal case where it is a *minimum* price that is being enforced. Maintenance of maximum prices is not contrary to the public interest; it is maintenance of minimum prices that causes waste.

the costs of small shopkeeping are high, and the rewards are correspondingly low, frequently much less than wage employment would yield. Neither is it a profession for the unskilled; the ignorance of small retailers is one of the principal reasons for their high rate of bankruptcy. In the United States it has been estimated that half the retail shops opened in any year fail within twelve months, and that the average life of a shop is only five years.[1] Similar information is not available for this country; thanks to price maintenance and a less aggressive atmosphere of competition the mortality rate is probably lower, but it is without doubt very high; to go into retailing is one of the easiest ways of losing the savings of a lifetime. Those who wish to keep retailing open specially to attract the small man seem therefore to be even more dangerous to the small man than they may be to the public.

It is more important to consider whether restricting the number of shops really would benefit the public. At present there is some competition in prices and in service. Restriction of entry might lead merely to an increase in shopkeepers' profits and prices, and to a decline in the quality of the service. The war has taught us how quickly the quality of the service deteriorates in retailing when once the spur of competition is removed, and many members of the public would think that some excess in the number of shops is a small price to pay in order to secure the benefits of competition.

The structure of the distributive trades would also be gravely affected by restriction of entry. For the past century the efficiency of retailing has been improving largely through the expansion of large-scale retailing—co-ops, multiples and department stores—relatively to small-scale retailing. Large-scale retailing is able to operate on margins of anything between 30 per cent and 50 per cent less than those required by small retailers. The small retailer has, indeed, his place in the industry, especially in the sale of shopping goods, where standardisation is not important, and in the sale of convenience goods in small shopping centres, and especially in building up a clientele on the basis of a high quality of personal service. This place would be even larger than it is if the efficiency of small shopkeepers could be improved, e.g. by better training facilities. A woeful ignorance of business principles is one of the chief causes of the wastefulness of small shopkeeping and the high mortality rate. For example, most small shopkeepers

[1] Temporary National Economic Committee, Monograph No. 17, *Problems of Small Businesses*, esp. Ch. II.

try to carry too wide a range of styles, brands, etc., deal with too many wholesalers and manufacturers, and offer too much service, for the limited turnover which they can secure. And the small man would be still more certain of his place if he would turn his eyes from the illusory safety of price maintenance and "classification" to the possibilities of standardisation and co-operative buying, thus challenging the large-scale retailer on his own ground. There is undoubtedly room for small-scale retailing. But what case is there for measures which extend it an artificial protection by preventing the expansion of large-scale retailing, which has been the spearhead of improved efficiency in distribution? The writer is as sensitive as any, and more sensitive than most, to the values of a society in which economic power is widely dispersed through the predominance of small business. But he is highly sensitive, too, to the persistence of poverty, and the need to increase wealth by utilising as far as possible the more productive types of enterprise. To bolster up small-scale retailing beyond its proper place in the distributive structure is to condemn an important part of our economy to waste and inefficiency. It should not be forgotten that one person in seven is engaged in the distributive trades.

More probably, this issue would not arise. For restriction of entry would give the multiples an incentive to buy up more and more small shops—small shopkeeping might not be preserved, but on the contrary might disappear. Nor would the public benefit; the small retailer, protected by his licence, would refuse to sell except for a handsome price, which the multiple organisation would be willing to pay, relying on the licence, and the net effect would be to raise prices against the public. Not only the multiples would play this game, but also the manufacturer. The public-house is a standing example of the incentive the licensing of retail outlets gives to manufacturers to integrate forward and buy up the outlets for monopolistic purposes. Probably the principal result of restricting entry into retailing would be that multiples and manufacturers would buy up the shops, that monopoly would be greatly increased in manufacturing, and that the public would lose more in higher prices and reduced service than it loses from freedom of entry. Though there are too many shops if there is freedom of entry, merely to restrict freedom of entry would probably make the public poorer than before.

4. What causes waste in retailing is not competition but the fact that price competition is not sufficiently effective, especially

in the convenience goods and suburban trades. This is due in the first instance to resale price maintenance, the abolition of which would enable the more efficient retailers to expand and to reduce prices to the consumer, and would reduce the number of shops, releasing resources for other urgent purposes.

But the number of shops might still be too large, and the average shop too small, even if price maintenance were abolished. Fig. I shows the position. In the absence of price competition the average shop will have a size well to the left of N (in terms of Fig. III it will be at K); price competition will increase the size to N; but the ideal size is given by M. Elasticity of demand will bring the competitive size nearer M, but not necessarily right up to it. Theoretically, the simple way to achieve the right number and size of shops is to fix a maximum gross margin QM, whereupon the number of shops will contract, and average size increase to M. But there is nothing simple about this solution in practice. There is in reality no average shop; different gross margins are appropriate in different conditions of population density and different degrees of service. The same margin cannot be fixed for every retailer. Neither is there an average commodity; even within a single class of merchandise different articles need different margins, according to the time it takes to handle them, their size, rate of turnover, and so on. It is true that margins have been elaborately controlled during the war, but no one can pretend that the hit or miss methods used in wartime would be very suitable for permanent peacetime regulation.

It may be suggested that the simplest way out is to fix a maximum margin only for one standard and popular type within each class of merchandise, in the expectation that the margins on all other types will have to correspond. This might work so long as retailers could not escape selling the selected brand. If "utility" production is continued, this can be tried, the Government allowing such low margins that only the appropriate number of shops remains in business. The retailers may be expected to fight the attempt by starting a whispering campaign against the "utility" articles, and persuading consumers to buy only uncontrolled articles. The Government would win so long as it retained power to withhold labour and raw materials from non-"utility" production, but as soon as non-"utility" lines could be freely produced, the limited price control would lose much of its effectiveness.

There is one other theoretical alternative to price fixing, which is equally impracticable, i.e. to give the co-operative societies a monopoly of retailing, or at least a monopoly of retailing convenience goods, since it is in these rather than shopping goods that there is excess capacity. If they had a monopoly of retailing the societies would have no incentive to establish more or less than the right number of shops. The proposal is specially attractive because, whatever their shortcomings in handling shopping goods, the co-operative societies are unquestionably the cheapest distributors of convenience goods in this country, and they would be cheaper still if certain managerial and structural reforms could be effected.[1] But it is politically quite impracticable to establish any such monopoly.

5. There is in fact no practicable solution to the problem of "excess capacity" in retailing, in the sense of reducing the gap between the competitive number and the ideal number of shops. This, however, need not daunt us, for two reasons. First because "excess capacity" exists only where elasticity of demand is insufficient to bridge the gap, on which we have no information. And secondly because, in either case, the actual number is so far in excess of the competitive number that if we could get it down to the competitive level we should have made notable progress. The way to this level is simply to make price maintenance illegal. This is the most urgent reform needed in retailing; its repercussions would revolutionise the distributive structure.

Democrats may rejoice that one result would be a rapid expansion of the consumers' co-operative movement in many trades for which it is specially suited. Here is a movement to which more than half the families in the country belong. Freed from the trammels of price maintenance, and inspired with a sense of its mission, this movement could set prices all along the line at levels which would drive waste out of distribution. It is the pride of the movement that it protected the consumer in the days when adulteration, short weight and fraud were the bugbear of retailing. To protect him from waste would add another page to an already noble history.

[1] For a discussion of needed reforms see Carr-Saunders and others, op. cit., especially Part IV.

CHAPTER VI

MONOPOLY AND THE LAW

AN ECONOMIST'S REFLECTIONS ON THE *CROFTER* CASE[1]

I

THE EVOLUTION OF THE LAW

How far apart economists and judges have travelled in their attitudes to monopoly: that is one's most striking impression on
reading the judgments in this case.[2] There was not always this
difference of view. The early judges abhorred monopoly no less
than does the economist; where the modern judge smiles beatific-
ally they grew apoplectic. The early history of the common law
shows no favour to trade combinations. In the earliest of these
cases, *R. v. Journeymen Tailors of Cambridge*,[3] the defendants were
convicted for criminal conspiracy, the court stressing that this was
an offence at common law. This view of trade combinations continued to be expressed for at least a century and a half. Lord
Mansfield stated it quite plainly in *R. v. Eccles*:[4]

"Persons in possession of any articles of trade may sell them
at such prices as they individually may please, but if they con-
federate and agree not to sell them under certain prices, it is
conspiracy."

So also in *R. v. Mawbey*,[5] *R. v. Hammond*,[6] *R. v. Bykerdike*,[7] *R. v.
Rowlands*,[8] *Hilton v. Eckersley*,[9] and *R. v. Druitt*,[10] though the
decision did not always turn on the point, judges went out of their

---

[1] This chapter was originally written for *The Modern Law Review* and
published in that journal in April 1943. The preceding issue had contained
the reflections of a lawyer on the same case, including a comparison of the
facts and legal arguments in this and other cases.

[2] *Crofter Hand Woven Harris Tweed Co., Ltd.* v. *Veitch and Another* (1942),
1 All E.R. 142.

[3] (1721), 8 Mod. 10.   [4] (1783), I Leach 274.

[5] (1796), 6 T.R. 619.   [6] (1799), 2 Esp. 719.

[7] (1832), I Moo. & R. 179.   [8] (1851), 17 Q.B. 671.

[9] (1855), 6 E. & B. 47; dicta of Crompton, J.   [10] (1867), 10 Cox 592

way to make it plain that trade combinations were a criminal conspiracy at common law. We know that at least some would-be conspirators were accordingly deterred; for when in 1852 the booksellers were contemplating a price-fixing association, and asked Lord Campbell's opinion, they disbanded themselves on his advising that such an association would render them liable to prosecution for criminal conspiracy.[1]

This position has now been abandoned. As early as 1815 pressure from trade conspirators for recognition of their agreements began to have its weight with some of the judges. In the criminal division they had little hesitation in pronouncing against conspiracies, because they wanted to leave no loophole for trade unions; in the civil division cases affected mainly business men's agreements, and the civil courts had begun to accept conspiracies between business men while the criminal courts were still rejecting conspiracies between their workers. As the legislature gradually extended its protection to trade unions, the urgency of declaring against trade conspiracies seemed to diminish.[2] By the last decade of the nineteenth century the capitulation was complete. The *Mogul* case[3] is the decisive watershed. Since that case, English judges have decided that business men[4] are to be free to enter into whatever combinations are necessary for the protection and advancement of their private trade interests. The public interest, on which the prohibition of conspiracy had rested, has been dethroned from its original place as the deciding factor. Lord Esher's last stand in the *Mogul* case, affirming the combination to be unlawful as against public policy, was not supported by his colleagues in the Appeal Court or by his superiors in the Lords. In the criminal courts no common law prosecution for trade conspiracy could now succeed. In actions in tort, Lord Cave's two propositions:

"(1) A combination of two or more persons wilfully to injure a man in his trade is unlawful and, if it results in damage to him,

---

[1] M. Plant, *The English Book Trade*, p. 439.

[2] Up to 1875 the decisions accepting conspiracies were *Hearn* v. *Griffin* (1815), 2 Chitty 407; *Wickens* v. *Evans* (1830), 3 Y. & J. 318; *R.* v. *Selsby* (1847), 5 Cox 495; *Shrewsbury and Birmingham Railway Company* v. *London & North Western Railway Company* (1851), 21 L.J.Q.B. 89; and *Hare* v. *London & North Western Railway Company* (1861), 2 J. & H. 80.   [3] (1892) A.C. 25.

[4] They had still not finally decided how much protection to give to workmen's combinations (*Quinn* v. *Leathem* (1901), A.C. 495), or to co-operatives (*McEllistrim* v. *Ballymacelligott Co-operative and Dairy Society*, (1919) A.C. 548).

is actionable. (2) If the real purpose of the combination is, not to injure another, but to forward or defend the trade of those who enter into it, then no wrong is committed and no action will lie, although damage to another ensues"[1]

will exculpate a combination for almost anything it is likely to do. And in the law of contract, practically all their agreements will receive the enforcement of the courts. Public policy is still occasionally mentioned, but how little consideration it receives can be judged from the observation of the Judicial Committee of the Privy Council in *Attorney-General of Australia* v. *Adelaide Steamship Company*[2] that—

"Their Lordships are not aware of any case in which a restraint, though unreasonable in the interests of the parties, has been held unenforceable because it involved some injury to the public."

The *Crofter* case reveals how far we have now been led. We knew before that a combine could charge whatever prices it saw fit and hold the public to ransom without interference from the courts. We knew that the court would help it discipline its members by compelling them to obey its rules, however anti-social those rules might seem. We knew that it was free to ruin any outside trader who did not accept its dictates. Now we discover new freedoms. Business men seeking to advance their private trade interests may not only combine with each other, but also bring their workers into the scheme, and promise them part of the swag; even this was hardly in doubt after the decision in *Reynolds* v. *Shipping Federation, Ltd.*[3] Now we know that they may use not only their own workers, but workers in any other industry who happen to belong to the same union. The trader or manufacturer who wishes to keep outside the conspiracy may find himself boycotted by every worker in his district. The householder who prefers Danish bacon to British may find that, at the behest of British farmers, the agricultural workers have persuaded the transport workers not to take him to his office, the laundry workers not to wash his clothes, the shop assistants not to sell to him, and so on, provided that they all belong to the same general union.

---

[1] *Sorrel* v. *Smith*, (1925) A.C., at p. 712.
[2] (1913) A.C. 781.   [3] (1924) 1 Ch. 28.

II

THE CASE AGAINST COMPETITION

Why did the judges go back on their original opinion? It is easy, if disrespectful, to picture them as pawns of the capitalist class, serving their masters' wishes even at the cost of the public good; easy, but not adequate. Doubtless some judges, consciously or unconsciously, have acted in the light of their inner conviction that the business man is the pillar of society and that law must serve and protect his ends. But the language to which they give expression is far more subtle than this. Most of the judgments which most strongly support combination are also those which in the strongest language insist on the freedom of the individual to trade on whatsoever terms he please. What has happened is a confusion of the different meanings of a single phrase. The free trade economists were clear enough what they meant by freedom of trade; to them it meant the absence of restraints on prices, emanating whether from Government or from private agreement, whether directly by price-fixing, or indirectly by curtailment of supplies. To them freedom meant freedom to enter the market and sell; not freedom to prevent others from so doing; or even freedom to barter away one's right of entry (of which the freedom to sell oneself into slavery is only the most extreme form). The judges confused these freedoms; have chosen to support the second and third, and therefore have become powerful agents in restraining the first. Some may have done this with a deliberate desire to advance the interests of their friends and heroes in the world of big business; most seem merely to have been confused; finding themselves called to deliver judgments on subjects they were never equipped to understand, they threw in their lot with what appeared to them to be the most modern developments. We must remember the atmosphere in which these cases are tried; though the decision is supposed to rest on what is or is not in the public interest, the courts admit no evidence on public policy.

"The question whether a restraint of trade is reasonable either in the interest of the parties or interest of the public is a question for the court, to be determined after construing the contract and the circumstances existing when it was made. It is really a question of public policy and not a question of fact upon which evidence of the actual or probable consequences, if the contract be carried into effect, is admissible."[1]

As Lord Bramwell commented—

"No evidence is given in these public policy cases. The tribunal is to say, as a matter of law, that the thing is against public policy and void. How can the judge do that without any evidence as to its effect and consequences?"[2]

He is left to work things out for himself from first principles, never having been trained to analyse such economic problems, and it is not surprising that he has gone astray.

Nevertheless, the line of reasoning which began as a defence of freedom has not been content to stay there. By degrees judges came out more and more openly as opponents of competition and supporters of monopoly as a way of life for Britain. There is a long line of *dicta* from the days of Ellenborough, C.J., who upheld a price-fixing agreement on the ground that—

"This is merely a convenient mode of arranging two concerns which might otherwise ruin each other,"[3]

to modern times, when Lord Haldane calmly assures us—

"Unquestionably the combination in question was one the purpose of which was to regulate supply and keep up prices. But an ill-regulated supply and unremunerative price may, in point of fact, be disadvantageous to the public. Such a state of things may, if it is not controlled, drive manufacturers out of business, or lower wages, and so cause unemployment and labour disturbance."[4]

And Scrutton, L.J., says—

"In view of the fluctuating character of the yearly supply of hops I see nothing unreasonable in hop-growers combining to secure a steady and profitable price, by eliminating competition amongst themselves, and putting the marketing in the hands of one agent, with full power to fix prices and hold up supplies, the benefit and loss being divided amongst the members."[5]

[1] Lord Parker in the *Adelaide* case (*supra*), at p. 797.
[2] In the *Mogul* case (*supra*), at p. 45.
[3] *Hearn* v. *Griffin* (1815) (*supra*), at p. 407.
[4] *North Western Salt Co.* v. *Electrolytic Alkali Co., Ltd.*, (1914) A.C. 467.
[5] *English Hopgrowers, Ltd.* v. *Dering*, (1928) 2 K.B. 174.

These judges do not merely say that they have no legal power to suppress monopoly; they go rather out of their way to make it clear that they consider monopoly to be in the public interest.

Judges are not unique in holding this view. The fervent belief in the virtues of competition which characterised the Britain of pre-1914 has died. The man in the street, no less than his rulers, has come to believe that competition is outmoded and anti-social, and that its speedy replacement serves the common weal. We have to decide whether this belief is justified or not. If it is acceptable, the judges are to be congratulated for being among the first to recognise a great truth. If it is rejected, a whole programme of legislative reform is needed to cope with the mischief they have done.

It is easy to show how fallacious are some of the arguments used in support of monopoly. Simplest of all is the fallacy that because monopoly benefits some, therefore it benefits all. Even learned judges have succumbed to this; it is implicit in the three passages just quoted; here again is Lawrence, L.J., arguing that the public is not injured if it is asked to pay more—

"Moreover, even in such a case, the mere intention to raise prices would not establish a case of injury to the public; it would still have to be proved that the intention was to raise prices to an unreasonable extent; for no such intention would be inferred, the reason being that *prima facie* it would be highly improbable that the seller in his own interest would want to fix unreasonable prices."[1]

The fact is that any increase in price makes the consuming public poorer, since it now has less money to spend on other things. As Adam Smith wrote in a classic passage, as long ago as 1776—

"The interest of the dealers, however, in any particular branch of trade or manufactures, is always in some respects different from, and even opposite to, that of the public. To widen the market and to narrow the competition, is always the interest of the dealers. To widen the market may frequently be agreeable enough to the interest of the public; but to narrow the competition must always be against it, and can serve only to enable the dealers, by raising their profits above what they would naturally be, to levy, for their own benefit, an absurd tax upon the rest of their fellow citizens. The proposal of any

[1] *Palmolive Co. (of England)* v. *Freedman*, (1928) 1 Ch. 264.

new law or regulation of commerce which comes from this order, ought always to be listened to with great precaution, and ought never to be adopted till after having been long and carefully examined, not only with the most scrupulous, but with the most suspicious attention. It comes from an order of men, whose interest is never exactly the same with that of the public, who have generally an interest to deceive and even to oppress the public, and who accordingly have, upon many occasions, both deceived and oppressed it."[1]

This is advice that every judge should take to heart.

There are, however, more subtle fallacies. One is that monopoly substitutes order and co-operation for chaos and antagonism. The view that there is no order in a competitive system appeals to those who, because they cannot actually see the wheels turning round, cannot realise that there are nevertheless powerful controls which operate it, to make it serve the consumer. Indeed, the true meaning of "to compete" is "to offer the public a substitute"; to serve the will of the market is the essence of competition. It involves antagonism in the sense that it allows the man in the street freedom to oppose business men to each other; to choose what he shall have and who shall serve it to him. Business men dislike this; it forces them to be efficient, and to be moderate in their prices. They see that by co-operating with each other they can take away from the man in the street his only means of subordinating them to his will —his freedom to choose between them, which compels them to seek his favours. Competition ended, the masses must take what their masters allow them. Competition has given way to co-operation if you like, but it is only co-operation between the few for the enslavement of the many.

Does not monopoly, however, reduce the insecurity of the economic system? Did not excessive competition characterise those two terrible decades from 1920, when the fear of unemployment hung like a cloud over millions of lives, and its reality broke so many thousands? Monopoly does, indeed, bring security for the few who are inside it; Lord Haldane is quite right to say that in its absence prices in some industries would fall; what he forgets is that the money the public saves in this way it can spend on buying the goods of other industries, thus increasing employment there. Competition cannot cause a slump. Neither can monopoly

[1] *The Wealth of Nations* (Cannan's Edition), Vol. I, p. 250.

either prevent slumps or cure them. It transfers income from poor to rich, and therefore, if anything, reduces employment by withdrawing money from those who would spend it and keep the wheels of industry turning, to those who characteristically save most. It is a complete fallacy to believe that competition causes the standard of living to be lowered; exactly the opposite is true.[1] The lean years were associated with competition, but competition was not their cause. Men swallow the fallacy because they associate slumps with low prices, and booms with high prices. Monopoly may keep prices stable, and may keep them high, but in doing so merely makes some richer and others poorer. There is a world of difference between high prices due to monopoly and high prices due to the great demand of men in employment in prosperous times. We cannot stabilise the demand, the employment and the prosperity simply by stabilising the prices.

The real cause of our difficulties in the past quarter of a century has been the absence of full employment; the real remedy lies not in the suppression of competition but in the maintenance of aggregate demand. Given full employment, everyone has opportunities of making a living, and it is not only desirable but imperative that he should justify the rewards he receives by being made to stand up to the competition of rival suppliers. If business men then combine to eliminate competition they can certainly secure higher earnings than they would otherwise, but they do so only at the expense of the public; to assume that if they profit the public also must gain is the most elementary of fallacies.

The case against competition is not, however, composed entirely of fallacies. All social institutions are imperfect, and competition is no exception.

There are two important classes of circumstance in which the effects of competition may be undesirable.

The first of these is where an industry whose equipment and labour force are highly specialised is suffering from long-term excess capacity. Suppose, for example, that the demand for the products of an industry contracts sharply, as in the British cotton, shipbuilding and coal industries after 1920, and that there is no

---

[1] If the monopoly is in an export trade it may be in a position to raise the standard of living at home by exploiting the foreign consumer; but few export industries are able to do this since in foreign markets they usually have to face the competition of other foreign exporters. A monopoly in an export industry usually exploits rather the domestic consumer.

prospect, as far ahead as one can see, of the industry's plant being fully utilised. It is then desirable that the surplus resources, men and equipment be transferred to other industries. Competition works to bring this about. Prices, wages, profits and other incomes in the industry fall to low levels, and pressure is thereby exerted on resources to transfer themselves elsewhere. The trouble is that if the resources are highly specialised it is very difficult to make the transfer. Then for years the situation drags on. All associated with the industry are impoverished, and they may try by trade combination to keep prices up as much as possible in order that their incomes should not sink too low. A trade combination for these purposes is obviously not so wicked as one designed simply to secure power to dominate the market. Nevertheless it does not contribute to the basic problem, which is to find employment elsewhere for the surplus resources which are acting as a drag on the market. What is really needed is positive action by the Government to promote industrial mobility. The industry needs a sharp surgical operation which, by adjusting supply to demand, can fit it once more to be restored to normal control by competition. This type of situation, while not remedied by the trade combination, does secure it greater sympathy. But it is the exception, and not the rule; in the cases so far brought before the courts it could seldom be argued that there was a severe and intractable problem of excess capacity to mitigate the offence.

The second case in which competition has undesirable effects is where the market is so limited in relation to the economies of large-scale production that there is really room only for one firm, or at most for two or three. Competition in these cases is not necessarily undesirable; it may, on the contrary, be the means by which one firm gains ascendancy in the market and attains the size at which the full benefit of the economies of scale can be obtained; the revolutionary effects of the entry of Henry Ford into the American automobile industry forty years ago is the standing proof that competition in price is frequently the quickest way to secure the economies of large-scale production. The danger in these cases is the possibility of a stalemate; when the firms, sharing the market in more or less equal portions, compete not by driving prices down to the minimum, in a fight to the death, but by differentiating their products and foregoing the benefits of standardisation, and by multiplying their sales staffs and otherwise adding to selling costs. The truth is that competition works well only where the market is so large relatively to possible economies of scale that there is room for a large number of producers. In other cases it tends to promote waste by multiplying the number of firms, the types of product, and the costs of distribution.

But even here the remedy is not the trade combination. What is needed in this sort of situation is that the number of firms should be reduced, unnecessary costs eliminated, and prices reduced. But what the combination does is to preserve the number of firms, by guaranteeing to each its quota, and to raise the price, or at least to keep it at a level adequate to maintain all the existing firms. If the firms were to amalgamate into a single unit, substantial economies could be achieved; redundant plant could be eliminated, and also duplication of selling costs. But this is quite a different proposition from a combination in which the firms retain their separate identities and merely share the market. Everything here rests on making the right distinctions. There is competition and competition; what is needed is competition in price, which almost always brings desirable results in the end, though the way may be painful; whereas competition in advertising, or in number of salesmen, or in product differentiation is frequently not in the public interest. Similarly there is monopoly and monopoly; the monopoly of a single large firm, securing the economies of scale, is frequently desirable, whereas the monopoly which consists of an agreement between separate firms to share out the market between them is most usually contrary to the public interest.

There is no doubt that this confusion in the public mind secures for monopoly an unmerited support. The impressive performance of monopoly is its technical achievement. We think of monopolists as owners of large factories working on a tremendous scale with wonderful machines with which workers can do in a day what others do in months. There is no doubt that there are industries where the economies of large-scale production are great, and where large monopolistic concerns are therefore able to produce more cheaply than small competitive establishments. This is beyond question; and so is its corollary that any law which tried to make the emergence of these concerns impossible would be a handicap to economic progress.

But what has this to do with trade combinations? We fall into error unless we distinguish sharply between the kind of monopoly where one firm by its size dominates the market, and that other kind where a number of firms enter into agreement to restrict output and maintain prices. The former may be associated with economies of large-scale production; the latter is not. In the sort of arrangement which is typified by the facts in the *Mogul* case, the *Adelaide* case, the *Salt* case, the Motor Trade Association cases,[1] or in *Joseph Evans* v. *Heathcote*,[2] there is no increase in productive efficiency. There may be some small economies in selling costs; but in so far as they result from diminishing the buyer's freedom of choice, they are not necessarily desirable; and they are in any case usually swamped by the loss of efficiency on the productive side. For a trade combination usually reduces productive efficiency, and this not merely because the stimulus to efficiency, competition, is removed. The whole *raison d'être* of such a combination is usually to prevent the firms with low costs from bringing prices down to the detriment of those with high costs; it usually allocates quotas, preventing the expansion of the low-cost firms, and enabling the inefficient to continue in production. It is a device which simultaneously robs the public and protects the inefficient. Whatever there may be to say in favour of the large firm, there is nothing to be said in favour of trade combinations. However well-meaning the judges may have been, they opened a door which could result only in the public detriment.

III

AIDS TO MONOPOLY

So much for trade combinations; what of that other form of monopoly where a firm by its size comes to dominate the market?

It is true that the emergence of such giants sometimes results in increased efficiency; but we must not too easily be deceived. In the first place, we must not conclude that the desirable pattern for all industry is necessarily the industrial giant. The fact is that the economies of large-scale production are greater in some industries than in others. Pig iron is most efficiently produced on a large scale; specialised steels are as cheaply produced by the small firm. The assembly of motor cars calls for large factories; the manu-

---

[1] *Ware & De Freville, Ltd.* v. *Motor Trade Association*, (1921) 3 K.B. 40; *Hardie & Lane, Ltd.* v. *Chilton*, (1928) 2 K.B. 306; and *Thorne* v. *Motor Trade Association*, (1937) A.C. 797, overruling *R.* v. *Denyer*, (1926) 2 K.B. 258.

[2] (1915) 1 K.B. 418.

facture of most of the parts to be assembled is efficiently done on a small scale. To run a regular liner service in shipping demands size; tramp shipping is easily done with very limited funds. The number of cases in which large firms are notably more efficient than small is not in fact great; over most of industry the small firm can produce as cheaply as the large. Technical economies are not so great as is supposed; very many large firms are using the same machines as small ones; only they are using more of them. And even where there are technical economies they may well be offset by the administrative difficulties involved in trying to co-ordinate the activities of a large concern, and to minimise the ever-present risk of bureaucratic inflexibility. In most industries, then, large scale confers no economies; in these monopoly has nothing to offer which competition would not be much more likely to secure.

Secondly, we must not lightly assume that all firms which grow in size are to be welcomed as torch-bearers of efficiency; nothing of the sort. This would only be the case if efficiency were the sole basis of expansion. But the fact is that many inefficient firms are able to grow by taking advantage of defects in our social organisation. A firm which has grown because it produces cheaply is to be welcomed; but a firm which has grown solely because it has bought up all the deposits of some essential mineral used by its industry, or all the outlets which the State will license, as in the case of breweries, or all the essential patents; or a firm which has grown by using financial strength to strangle its competitors—such a firm is not necessarily deserving of praise. Monopoly is too great a source of power for us to accept its emergence save on grounds of the strictest purity. As the late Professor Allyn Young has written—

"Most of the more weighty discussion of the economic advantages of monopoly have to do with the effect of monopoly upon the aggregate production of wealth measured in terms either of subjective satisfaction or of objective commodity units. Even from this point of view the case for monopoly is exceedingly dubious, and at best, has a validity that is restricted and conditioned in many ways. Moreover, such considerations are relatively unimportant compared with matters like the effect of monopoly upon distribution, upon the scope for individual initiative, upon economic opportunity in general, and upon a host of social and political relations. In short, it is a question less of the relative 'economy' of monopoly or competition than of the kind of economic organisation best calculated to give us the kind of society we want. Until our general social ideals are radically changed, it will take more than economic analysis to prove that it would be sound public policy to permit monopoly in that part of the industrial field where competition is possible."[1]

On the purely economic issues most monopolists hasten to assure us that they intend to keep their undertakings up to the highest pitch of efficiency, and that they will not use their power to exploit the public. But the issue of monopoly is not just a question of whether prices are to be high or low, and output large or small, important as these matters are in a world as poor as ours still is. It is even more a question of opportunity. The spread of monopoly is the spread of privilege; opportunity is denied to those who are outside the ring. In nineteenth-century Britain, men with initiative could rise in industry; in the twentieth century they are locked out, unless they are the sons or favourites of the industrial barons who have assumed control over the country's major industries. A new hereditary industrial aristocracy has replaced the old heredi-tary landed aristocracy; and the brief vision of democracy which early capitalism seemed to be bringing in the nineteenth century has vanished. The rise of monopoly has meant a concentration of control over great aggregations of wealth in the hands of a few men; in nearly every British industry one man or two, in his own name or that of the ring he represents, can take decisions which may plunge thousands into unemployment, put prices beyond the range of thousands more, suppress new inventions, or ruin all the carefully laid plans of some local authority. The power they possess may be well exercised, but it is arbitrary power. In the nineteenth century we learnt to reject power over society without control by society in the political field; the twentieth is teaching that it is no less vicious in the economic field.

Let us therefore examine more closely some of the steps on which a firm may climb to power without necessarily being efficient. They are not all associated with defects in the law. Thus one of these steps is the superior financial facilities available to large firms. The situation is not as bad here as it is in the United

---

[1] "The Sherman Act and the New Anti-trust Legislation," *Journal of Political Economy*, Vol. XXIII (1915), p. 214.

States of America. There big business and banking are indissolubly linked, and denial of finance a major means of strangling the small firm. In this country banks are more closely confined to short-term finance; firms are not dependent on them for capital; and their power to strangle is much less. But the small firm does meet unnecessary difficulties in raising capital, compared with the facilities available to large firms. The Macmillan Committee recommended in 1931 that this situation should be remedied. If there were adequate sources of finance for small firms, such as a Government financial corporation might provide, they would keep alive more easily, and the big firm would not so easily gobble them up. Another device for rising to power is mass advertising. It is not a very secure method, since advertised products compete with one another, and have in addition to face the competition of unadvertised products bought by those members of the public who, for a guarantee of quality, rely more on the advice of their regular retailer than on what they read in newspaper advertisements. Advertising is the reason for the existence of some large firms, but the case against it does not rest primarily on its rôle as a source of monopoly power. Rather does it rest on the fact that it does not seem to serve any social purpose useful enough to justify the £100,000,000 a year spent on it. Proposals to confine advertising to trade periodicals certainly deserve sympathetic hearing.

Turn, however, to the defects in the law which aid would-be monopolists. The first of these is in the patent law. The theory underlying the grant of the patent privilege is that it is a reward for the inventor: he is entitled for a number of years to a royalty on any use of his invention. In fact, however, the existing patent law confers a privilege not only on the inventor, but also on the user. A firm may buy the patent, and with it the right to exclude all other firms from using the invention, however willing they may be to pay the inventor his royalty. Thus a rich firm can buy up all the most essential inventions in its industry and dominate the market; those inventions which challenge its invested capital it may suppress. Reform this situation, and a number of monopolies would dissolve. Make all patents "licence of right," giving any firm the right to use the invention on paying a royalty to the inventor. This might mean that some doubtful inventions would not be tried out on a commercial scale, since no firm would sink money in the experiment unless assured that only it would benefit;

but this is not likely to be common, and any social loss through this source would be more than compensated by ending a system under which valuable inventions are suppressed and delayed, and others used to exploit the public. The Patent Acts have tried to prevent the abuse of patents by giving special powers to the Comptroller of Patents; but experience shows that large abuses call for drastic remedies.

A second defect is that the law permits boycotts and insistence on exclusive dealing. If strong enough, a firm may use a boycott to kill a rival, either by threatening its customers, or by threatening its suppliers. An example of the former is the *Shoe Machinery* case,[1] where the firm insisted on exclusive dealing, penalising customers who wanted to do part of their business with its rivals. The courts have not been presented with a case illustrating the use of boy- cotts on supplies by a single firm, though there are many cases of its use by trade combinations, as in *Sorrel's* case and the Motor Trade Association cases. Could there be any clearer example of an attempt to restrain trade than the use of the boycott? Yet the Privy Council dismissed the *Shoe Machinery* case on the ground that—

"By virtue of the privilege which the law secures to all traders, namely that they shall be left free to conduct their own trade in the manner which they deem best for their own interests, so long as that manner is not in itself illegal, the respondents are at liberty to hire or not to hire the appellants' machines as they choose, irrespective altogether of the injury their refusal to deal may inflict on others. The same privilege entitles the appellants to dispose of the products they manufacture on any terms not in themselves illegal, or not to dispose of their products at all, as they may deem best in their own interest, irrespective of like consequences. This privilege is indeed the very essence of that freedom of trade in the name and in the interest of which the respondents claim to escape from the obligations of their contracts."[2]

Is not this passage of the very essence of that confusion between freedom to trade, freedom to restrain trade, and freedom to dis- pose of one's own freedom to trade, to which the judges have proved so prone? And the cases where firms have got suppliers to

---

[1] *United Shoe Machinery Co.* v. *Brunet*, (1909) A.C. 330.
[2] Ibid., at pp. 342–3.

withhold supplies from a rival, instead of being discussed in terms of the desirability or otherwise of this form of restraint of trade, have been made, by some peculiar legal quirk, to hang on the test of conspiracy; curious exercises have been made to show why a boycott engineered by two in combination is worse than a boycott engineered by one giant—the judgments explaining away *Quinn* v. *Leathem* and justifying *Allen* v. *Flood* would make amusing reading were they not so tragic—and after all this the offenders have got away on the ground that their conspiracy was only to promote legitimate trade interests. There was, indeed, some point in the question whether the restraint involved in tying a customer or supplier to a particular firm is an unreasonable restraint. If X contracts to serve as Y's secretary for a year, and to serve no other person during that time, or if A agrees to sell all his output to B, there is a restraint on the freedoms of X and A to enter their respective markets. But it is not necessarily an undesirable restraint. It becomes such only in the hands of a monopolist, for he alone can use it as a device for strangling rivals. The law might well permit such contracts to firms which cannot exploit them, while denying them to others in a monopolistic position. The attempt to apply this principle to one kind of monopolist, the possessor of a patent, failed because when the Bill passed from the House of Commons to the House of Lords, their Lordships so mutilated the relevant section as to render it practically useless. What we need now is a well-drafted clause applying to all monopolists.

A third defect in the law is that it permits price discrimination. Would-be monopolists flourish by extorting special prices and rebates from their suppliers to the detriment of smaller rivals; and they conquer small markets often by temporarily lowering the price there until the local firm is driven out of business; the use of "fighting ships" in the *Mogul* case was an example of this. Price discrimination is another device which, though harmless in the hands of small firms, can be deadly in the hands of monopolists. Parliament has recognised this, and in most cases where it creates monopoly it controls price discrimination—on the railways, in electricity supply and in the hands of other public utilities. What is lacking is the realisation that monopolies which do not emerge with Parliamentary backing are even worse than those which do, and that therefore their actions need even greater control.

These defects in the law all point in one direction. If it is accepted that the giant concern can only be tolerated where its size is based on efficiency, and that monopoly on any other basis is bad, then it follows that the law ought positively to remove all undesirable aids to size. In the nineteenth century it was taken for granted, more or less, that the market could look after itself. This was obviously untrue of some markets, like transport or gas, but these were taken as exceptions, and special provision was made for them as public utilities. What is now clear is that all markets have to work within a certain legal framework, and that unless the framework is adequate, the market will cease to be free. To keep the market as free as possible should be a positive task of the law. How far is this possible?

IV

LESSONS FROM AMERICA

It is now commonly believed that American experience has proved the futility of any attempt to control monopoly by law. "See," we are told, "America is the country with the most determined anti-trust legislation, and yet nowhere else are there more powerful monopolistic corporations." On this there are several things to be said.

The first is, that if American experience proves anything, what it proves most is that no law can succeed unless the means are provided for enforcing it. When the Sherman Act was passed it seems to have been expected to operate largely through private parties bringing suits against monopolies. Business men injured by combinations would set it in motion for the recovery of triple damages. Accordingly only very small sums were set aside for public enforcement. In Theodore Roosevelt's day the anti-trust division had only five lawyers; in the 1920's the number never exceeded twenty-five; not until 1938 did it reach fifty. Private enforcement has proved inadequate—apart from anything else it is much too expensive a procedure. Accordingly in 1939 the other Roosevelt multiplied the sums at the disposal of the division; its staff of lawyers reached two hundred; for the first time the division was able to prepare its cases properly and to make a wide assault on monopoly. The results of this action leave no doubt that anti-trust legislation can be a most effective deterrent of monopolists, and save the public millions of dollars. The first lesson for us, therefore, is that, desirable as it may be to encourage actions in tort to compensate for injuries inflicted, major reliance should be placed on enforcement by a Government department with adequate funds. Rather a special kind of Government department is required: our traditional repository for powers of this kind, the Board of Trade, has not the machinery. It must be a department with police powers, including men capable of nosing out restraints from the conflicting evidence of witnesses and files of complicated papers; a department with economists trained to analyse the pattern of an industry and the effects of its peculiar restraints; and a department with lawyers, able to present a good case. We need a special "Department of Monopoly Control."[1]

That is the administrative side of American experience. What of the legal side? Can the law really maintain competition? The answer to this is in two parts, corresponding to the two different types of monopoly, the single giant and the trade combination.

American experience does indeed prove that it is useless to try to prevent rival firms from merging into big corporations. Much of the confusion, and most of the disappointment associated with American anti-trust experience, have been due to the fact that the Sherman Act did not make plain whether such fusion was to be penalised or not. The Act prohibited monopolies and attempts to monopolise. At first the Supreme Court interpreted this in such a way as to forbid mergers that promoted monopoly; then it changed its mind. The Clayton Act was more specific, prohibiting big concerns from purchasing each other's shares, or even having interlocking directorates—but the corporation lawyers got round this: now one company buys not the shares but the physical assets of the other. If two concerns do not want to compete with each other, no law can compel them to, and it is futile to try to stop them from merging.

But while this is true of two big concerns determined to co-operate, it does not quite apply where a giant is trying to swallow a number of smaller rivals. It is a lot to ask the public to stand by and watch some magnate buying up all the cinemas, or all the pubs, with intent to create a monopoly, and to take no steps to

[1] Far and away the best appraisal of the administrative problems involved is the monograph by W. H. Hamilton and I. Till, for the Temporary National Economic Committee, *Anti-trust in Action*, 1940; it contains also a valuable discussion of such problems as penalties and the enforcement of judicial orders. See also T. W. Arnold, *The Bottlenecks of Business*, New York, 1940.

stop him. Sometimes he will have a clear case in his favour, where the resulting reorganisation under a single control can bring substantial economies and lower costs and prices. But frequently there is no such case. There ought to be powers entitling the government to stop a monopolist from making further acquisitions where it cannot be shown that substantial economies will result. It is proposed, under Town and Country Planning legislation, that every time land use is to be changed a licence must be sought from public commissioners. It is not therefore too much to require—a much less frequent occurrence—that any firm which controls (or any large shareholder in a firm which controls) say one-third of the trade in any line of business should be prohibited from buying the assets or shares of rival concerns except under a licence, which would be granted only where substantial economies were expected to result.

This is the most difficult part of monopoly control, and is the part where American anti-trust legislation has clearly failed, through omitting provision for the exercise of administrative discretion. (A law which does not provide for the reasonable exceptions always breaks down.) In other important directions, however, anti-trust legislation has been amply successful. The Clayton Act (now reinforced by the Robinson-Patman Act) forbade exclusive dealing, boycotts and price discrimination, which, as we have seen, are important tools for monopoly-building. These prohibitions have been very effective despite defects in the drafting. One defect was that, since the Acts prohibit these devices "where the effect . . . may be to substantially lessen competition or tend to create a monopoly in any line of commerce," the courts were left to decide when this condition was fulfilled, and had to plunge into a mass of economic material which judges are not usually trained to interpret. The difficulty could be got round by denying these devices to monopolists, and defining a monopolist as "any person who has a patent,[1] copyright, trade mark, brand, licence or other privilege protected by the law; any person whose purchases or sales amount to one-third of the total sales of the commodity in the United Kingdom; or any person acting in combination with other buyers or sellers."[2] Another defect was that while the Clayton Act applied the prohibition to leases and to contracts

[1] If all patents were "licence of right," patentees could be omitted.
[2] Trade combinations need not be included if their formation is prohibited under some other clause.

of sale it omitted agency,[1] which thereby unnecessarily gave scope for evasion. A third defect was that instead of refusing to sell a commodity X unless the buyer bought also Y, an act forbidden by the law, a seller could put X and Y together, call them one commodity, and refuse to sell them apart;[2] this is another evasion which might easily be stopped up.

If in Britain we were to enact similar provisions to those in the Clayton and Robinson-Patman Acts directed against boycotts, exclusive dealing and price discrimination, and if we were simultaneously to revise the patent law, the market would take a new lease of freedom. Concerns would then have to rely primarily on efficiency as a means of growth. They would be surrounded almost always by numerous smaller rivals, with free and fearless access to supplies (except where these are limited mineral deposits) and to markets; the large firm could not boycott, and could make few gains not wholly deserved on the basis of efficiency. In many cases no further control would be needed to prevent exploitation. But in some cases, where the economies of large scale are marked, no small rivals could survive. Then the market would be at the mercy of one or two large giants, and more positive controls would be needed. They lie easy to hand; Parliament controls some monopolies by regulating their prices, e.g. electricity concerns, others by limiting their profits, e.g. gas concerns. In other cases there is operation by municipal authorities, by Government departments, or by specially created public corporations like the London Passenger Transport Board. Wherever the scale of production is too large for competition to survive, there should be machinery for public control. This is a well-established tradition in Great Britain, only we have limited its application to a narrow field that we choose to call "public utility," and to one or two other special cases, such as the rather inadequate supervision of the Import Duties Advisory Committee over iron and steel prices; what we need now is to extend the principle of public utility control to all cases where the economies of scale must supersede competition.[3]

So much for the giant concern. What does American experience

---

[1] *Federal Trade Commission* v. *Curtis Publishing Co.*, 260 U.S. 568 (1923).

[2] *Federal Trade Commission* v. *Gratz et al.*, 253 U.S. 421 (1920).

[3] If all these large concerns were controlled as to profits and prices or publicly operated they might perhaps be excluded from the prohibition of exclusive dealing, since this method of trade is sometimes beneficial, and is only harmful in the hands of uncontrolled monopolies.

teach about the attempt to prevent rings and combinations between the smaller fry? This, after all, is the type of monopoly much more common in the United Kingdom than is the industrial giant, though of those we have also our share. Here the interpretation of the law provided little difficulty; the Supreme Court wavered only once,[1] and not for long. The experience is overwhelmingly conclusive that trade combinations are easy to smell out, and that their suppression presents little practical difficulty.

Properly to understand what is possible, we must begin by analysing markets into three types. At one extreme are those where the scale of operation is so small that the number of firms is very large, e.g. in this country cotton spinning, road haulage, or retail trade. In such markets no voluntary agreement is stable; the numbers concerned are too large; and a minority will always blackleg and spoil the fun. Experience has proved that an agreement will survive only if the legislature intervenes to impose it on all firms. Competition in such cases has disappeared only because the State has prohibited it; even after war-time concentration, repeal of a dozen Acts would usually restore it in full vigour.

At the other extreme are markets which are so small, or where the scale of operations is so large, that agreement is inevitable and no law can prevent it. With these we have already dealt; anti-trust measures are futile; what is required are positive controls, whether price or profit limitation, or public operation.

The intermediate cases are the most difficult. Here the number of firms is large, but not too large for agreement. There is the inevitable minority which would ruin the agreement, but it can be boycotted. This is also where an anti-combination law is most useful. It can make the agreement a criminal conspiracy; refuse the enforcement of contracts; and give to injured minorities full damages (triple damages under the Sherman Act) at law. American experience shows that the existence of such a law makes it extremely difficult for such combinations to hold together effectively. They have of course sought means of evading it. Not all the acts of trade associations are vicious, and not all are prohibited. Those which need to be prohibited are the fixing of prices, the restriction of output, allocation of quotas, imposition of distance limits, compilation of stop lists or agreements express or implied with suppliers to withdraw supplies from outside firms. There are, however, legitimate activities—research, compilation of statistics,

---

[1] *Appalachian Coals, Inc.* v. *U.S.*, 288 U.S. 344 (1933).

promotion of standardisation, representation on public committees, etc. The difficulty arises where legitimate activities are
used for illegitimate purposes, as when an association circulates
information as to current prices or orders placed or output which
its members tacitly accept as indications what prices they should
charge or how far to restrict their output. The existence of this
possible loophole, however, is not very dangerous unless the group
is small enough to exclude blacklegs, or is able to penalise them
and get away with it in the courts. So also with that other evasion,
"price leadership." This is found where there is some large firm
dominant in an industry, surrounded by a number of smaller
rivals. There is no price agreement, but all firms take their cue
from the leader, and he, by virtue of his strength, exercises the
function of bringing recalcitrants into line. If all large firms were
publicly controlled this might solve the problem of "price leadership," but even without this the situation can be kept in hand,
provided there is an enforcing authority with its eyes open for cases
of boycott, exclusive dealing, or price discrimination, since these
are the weapons with which price leadership is enforced. If agreement is prohibited, the wings of the large firm clipped, and the
small firm encouraged, the market will keep free without much
difficulty.

What are the alternatives? Given that business men cannot be
left free to do as they please, there are two. One is the German
system; to recognise cartels with their quotas and minimum prices,
but to take power to supervise them, as under the *Kartellverordnung*
of November 1923. It is well known that this decree was never
seriously applied; but assuming that such a decree could be
enforced, and that it were possible adequately to supervise the
prices and quotas fixed by every single trade association, is this
the desirable alternative? To hold this view is to forget that
monopoly is not primarily a question of prices; it is even more a
question of efficiency, of initiative, of opportunity and of freedom
from concentrated power; these are the ends which competition
secures more effectively than any other form of organisation. To
reject competition and choose price regulated cartels is to miss
altogether the meaning of the problem. The other alternative,
some socialists would suggest, is nationalisation. Is it really an
alternative? Leaving out workers on their own account, there are
over a million separate commercial establishments in this country.
Is it a practical proposal for a Labour Government simultaneously

to take over every one of them? Surely, leaving aside the very big question whether such action would be desirable on its own merits, do not at least the administrative difficulties compel concentrating nationalisation on the most urgent cases, which, apart from industries nationalised for reasons of political strategy, are the cases where large-scale economies make monopoly inevitable? However distasteful he may find it, the Labour Prime Minister is bound to leave whole sectors of the economy to private enterprise while he concentrates his energies on key industries. He has therefore to decide whether it is to be monopolistic or competitive private enterprise. He may well want to keep the trade associations because their existence makes it easier to deal with the producers in an industry and to issue them their orders. But this does not mean that they must retain monopoly powers. Let them negotiate with Government, publish statistics, and do all the other legitimate activities of trade associations; but boycotts, price-fixing, quotas and all the other paraphernalia of monopoly must go. Private enterprise can only be retained in so far as it is competitive; in so far as it is retained it must be made to compete.

V

CONCLUSION

"If the monopoly established by the appellants and their mode of carrying on their business be as oppressive as is alleged (upon which their Lordships express no opinion) then the evil if it exists may be capable of cure by legislation or by competition, but in their view not by litigation"; thus the Privy Council in the *Shoe Machinery* case.[1] This article has sought to indicate the sort of legislation that is needed to carry on the good work which the judges so unfortunately abandoned. It may be summarised as follows:

(a) The maintenance of free markets is a positive task to which the police power of the State should be applied; this requires a special department, amply staffed.

(b) The Act under which such department operates should prohibit trade combinations, specifying the acts which are outlawed; and should deny to monopolists the right to buy up competitors and the use of boycotts, exclusive dealing

[1] *Supra* at p. 344.

and price discrimination, specifying what is meant by a monopolist.

(c) The patent law should be revised to make all patents "licence of right"; and

(d) The principles of public utility regulation or public operation should be extended to all industries where the economies of large-scale production necessarily result in the market being dominated by a few large concerns.

We cannot produce complete economic democracy simply by adopting this programme; there are many other points at which business needs to be regulated in the public interest. We need these provisions, however, at least as part of the programme if such private business as is retained after the war is to be made not the master but the servant of the public. This remains almost the only important country without legislation to keep the market free, or at least a general law to control the activities of monopolists. If private groups are not to submerge the public interest, Parliament must take bold action to control monopoly, and now is the time to decide what lines it should follow.

CHAPTER 7

THE ADMINISTRATION OF SOCIALIST ENTERPRISES

In the early days of socialist thought it was almost an axiom that once property passed from private hands to public ownership all the major social problems were automatically solved; it would be put to purposes conforming more to the public interest, income would be more equitably distributed, economic power would be democratised, efficiency would increase, and the class struggle between owners and workers would end. This view has not survived the experience. Half a century of municipal enterprise and twenty-five years of the public corporation have proved little more than that public operation has both advantages and disadvantages; that it offers new opportunities of solving old problems, but at the same time brings new problems of its own. Indeed, there is not a little disillusionment among some whose expectations were greatest. "We, the public," were to have managed our undertakings in the public interest; in practice, the Minister appoints a Board, headed by Lord X and including a galaxy of anti-socialist names, tells them to get on with the job, and leaves the public very much wondering what the social revolution was about. How to make the public corporation public has become the serious concern of socialist thinkers, and is a problem that all must share. Socialist enterprise has come to stay in Britain. Tories, Liberals and Socialists have all played their part in establishing the public corporation, and though they may quarrel in deciding how far to extend its sway, all are committed to it in principle, and all equally concerned to see that its operation shall really serve the public interest.

We, the public, cannot manage the affairs of a corporation; that must be done by its Board of Directors. We, or our representatives, can appoint the Board, and trust to luck that if we have appointed the right people we can just let them get on with the job. But of course there are no such right people; to criticise a socialist Government for appointing conservative Boards is wide of the mark if it implies that the problem would be solved merely by appointing men of different political complexion. There are no men, whatever their views or their abilities, who are good enough to be trusted with the management of the public's resources, and just left to carry on with the job; and it is odd that men who learnt this secret of democracy in their infancy, and take it for granted in central and local government, have been so blind to it in constructing plans for economic democracy. Democracy is made by vigilance, by rules, and by accountability. The success of the public corporation depends in the long run on how precisely and adequately we frame the rules which must govern its conduct.

From this the analysis of the problem follows logically. Section I elaborates the principle of accountability; Section II discusses policy; Section III efficiency; Section IV fair competition in partly socialised industries; and Section V sums up.

I

ACCOUNTABILITY

The public corporation must be accountable to the public for all its actions. The current dogma that the corporation must be "independent of political control" bids fair to ruin socialism by delivering us into the hands of a tyranny more deadly than has ever been conceived. It is incompatible with democracy that a small Board shall be given power over immense resources, over the lives of hundreds of thousands of workers and the satisfactions of millions of consumers, without formidable controls over their actions. That any idea of independence should ever have been introduced into the discussion of the public corporation has been a disaster, and may prove a disaster from which it will never recover. The corporations established before 1945 were not made responsible even to Parliament. Ministers answer certain questions, but they disclaim responsibility even in answering them, and questions have to be most carefully framed to get past the clerks of the House and on to the order paper. In one of them, the London Passenger Transport Board, the members of the Board are not even appointed by a Minister. This extreme quest for independence has now been abandoned. In the new corporations of the Labour Government, the Minister appoints the Board and reserves the right to give general directions.

At the same time, we must beware of tendencies to seek a

remedy in Parliamentary control. Parliamentary control of corporations is necessary, but it cannot get very far. Parliament has neither the time nor the knowledge which is necessary to control the affairs of public corporations. If John Smith is refused facilities for transporting his goods, or charged an unreasonable price; if the citizens of some small hamlet are denied a gas supply; if there is no bus service after 8 p.m.; if an employee is unjustly discharged—there are a thousand daily instances of dissatisfaction with the behaviour of public corporations, many of which ought to be investigated, and which must be investigated if the system is to give us not less democracy but more. Parliament cannot investigate them; it has neither time nor competence. Parliament can discuss general questions of principle, on infrequent occasions, and it can be a last resort on some point of detail, but for day-to-day control of corporations democracy must look elsewhere.

If John Smith is dissatisfied with facilities or with charges he will bargain first with the corporation. Every public corporation ought to have first class public relations contacts. This means not that the corporation should do a lot of advertising, but that it should have both facilities for taking the initiative in discovering what the public thinks and wants (market research), and also officers whose job it is to deal with complaints, not with a view to giving soft answers, but with real power inside the corporation to force departmental officers to accede to reasonable requests. A good internal organisation for public relations is the public's first line of defence. But it is only the first line of defence. Boards of Directors may neglect to have a good organisation, and cannot be compelled to it either by legislation or by ministerial order; the corporation may have adopted a bad policy which the public relations officers cannot get changed; or the corporation may be right and John Smith wrong, but it cannot be judge in its own case, and he is entitled to have an independent ruling. In railway transport there are two tribunals—shortly to be merged into one —to which he can take his case, and long experience has shown how important it is to have some such independent appeal.

Whenever a public corporation is established there should be established at the same time an expert tribunal to whom the public may refer complaints in respect of services or charges; and the decisions of such tribunals should be final on questions of fact, with limited appeal on questions of law.

A tribunal should be liable to motion from four sources. First, the individual customer should have the right to bring his complaint, with the usual legal proviso that he pays the cost of actions he loses, and is reimbursed if he wins. Such a proviso is needed to prevent frivolous actions; the danger that it will inhibit justifiable actions can be met by simplifying procedure, and by limiting the costs of an unsuccessful action. Secondly, if the complaint is one of general rather than particular interest, representative associations may move; trade associations, chambers of commerce, local authorities and similar bodies should be the second source of motions. Thirdly, statutory Consumers' Councils can be useful, and it is to such a tribunal that they should take issues on which they cannot reach agreement with the corporation. And fourthly, there is the Minister, who must have residual powers to put issues to the tribunal.

The current fashion is to rely instead on establishing Consumers' Councils as a substitute for tribunals; but they are altogether inadequate to the purpose. Members of a Consumers' Council can meet together at infrequent intervals and discuss general policy, and no doubt a corporation will pay attention to their pronouncements even without waiting for Ministerial intervention. But such Councils are not competent to do the sort of work which the Railway Rates Tribunal and the Railway and Canal Commission have had to do. They cannot make decisions on major issues, and they have not the time for John Smith's points of detail. Only expert tribunals of assessors are competent for this work, which raises difficult problems of law, economics, and accounting. A Consumers' Council has many useful functions of a general nature, to which we shall refer subsequently, but it is not a substitute for, but a supplement to a tribunal.

Even the tribunal has been attacked on the ground that some of the problems are so difficult that issues must be determined largely by the "hunch" of the corporation's Board. Difficulties and hunches are irrelevant. Someone has to make a decision, however difficult, and it cannot be democratic for the corporation to be judge in its own cause. The relevance of difficulties is that such tribunals must fail unless definite rules are laid down to guide their decisions. It is not enough to say that they must act "in the public interest." The public interest has to be defined as precisely as is possible, and to this task we now turn.

II

PRICE POLICY

A long tradition of public utility regulation has already established two principles for the guidance of tribunals on services and charges; namely the right of the individual customer to reasonable facilities on payment of the appropriate charge, and his right to be protected against undue preference being shown to others. A whole series of cases here and in other countries have elaborated their meaning.

In practice the most serious difficulties emerge from the demand for services which cannot pay for their cost. One of the most dangerous of current dogmas is the assertion that it does not matter if individual parts of the service provided by a corporation do not pay so long as total receipts cover total costs; many socialists actually argue that one of the advantages of nationalisation is that it makes it possible to charge for certain services well beyond their cost, and to use the profits on these services to subsidise others which cannot be self-supporting. Off-peak transport services are to be subsidised by peak travellers; peak electricity supply by off-peak users; consumers of transport or electricity or post office services living in rural or sparsely populated districts by those who live in congested areas; and so on. Fairness is thought to demand that every buyer should pay the same price, irrespective of differences in cost of supply, so the low cost supply must subsidise the high cost supply. So long as total receipts cover total costs, it is argued, it does not matter that some parts of the supply are not self-supporting.

There are even those who argue that necessaries should not be sold at all. Everyone should be free to have as much water, gas, electricity, bread, milk and other essentials as he requires without payment, the cost of supplies being defrayed from the general revenue.

Fairness does not take us very far in this dispute. It is not more fair that a man should pay irrespective of cost than that he should pay according to cost. But neither can economic analysis supply any settlement of the controversy. Consider the inhabitants of the hamlet of Little Misery, who live in a bleak and dismal spot on the ledge of a high hill, and whom it is exceptionally costly to supply with water, gas, electricity, frequent transport, bread, milk and postal services. There are arguments in favour of the community deciding that these unfortunate people should be helped by subsidy to the amenities of life; there are also arguments in favour of making the silly fatheads pay the full cost of choosing to remain in such an inaccessible spot. But they are not economic arguments, and economics cannot decide them. Again, if electricity is "put on to the rates", and supplied without charge, it is not open to question that much of it will be wasted, both in the sense that it will more often be left on when it is not required, and also in the sense that people will use it in cases where the benefit it confers to them is less than the cost of supply (so that if they were offered the choice between free electricity and a sum of money equal to the cost of what they would otherwise consume, they would prefer the money). Economists abhor waste, but there are arguments in favour even of waste, and economics cannot pronounce upon them.

Economic democracy contributes only three guiding principles. The first is that the community should know the cost of what it is doing, the second that it should be satisfied that this cost is equitably distributed, and the third that decisions should be made democratically. It is not obvious that the inhabitants of the hamlet of Little Misery should be subsidised, and there should surely be no general rule requiring public corporations to subsidise them. If some services are to be supplied below cost, each case must be considered on its merits. The general rule to corporations ought to be not to supply below cost, and if in particular cases people wish this rule to be waived they ought to be required to state their case to an appropriate authority. The public corporation is not itself the appropriate authority. The men appointed to the Boards of gas or electricity or transport concerns are appointed for their competence in these fields and not as proper judges of such issues as the general merits of Little Misery. Subsidy decisions require to be made by a democratically elected authority representing both the receivers and the payers of the subsidy, that is to say by local authorities for local issues, and by Parliament for national issues. Thus the constitution of a public corporation may give the Minister power, after appropriate discussion, to order the corporation to supply some particular service below cost. In the absence of such order the inflexible rule, binding alike on corporation and on price and service tribunal must be no service below cost.

But this is only the first stage. When the Minister decides to subsidise some particular class of consumers he must at the same time decide who should foot the bill. The general assumption of most socialist writers is that the cost should be levied on the other consumers of the service. The only argument in favour of this is that it may be convenient. If the Minister decides that schoolchildren and expectant mothers should get milk below cost it does not follow that the cost of milk ought to be raised to all other consumers; a subsidy from general revenues is usually considered to be more appropriate. There will be cases where financing by levying on all consumers is the best method, but there should be no general rule to this effect. When the Minister is deciding to order the subsidy, he must decide at the same time who is to foot the bill.

Now if the community is to be able to act rationally in these matters it must know the facts. In particular the accounts of public corporations must be published in such form that the cost of each part of the service can be compared with its revenue, and one of the duties of a Consumers' Council should be to examine the accounts with a view to establishing which parts of the undertaking are unprofitable. No public corporation in this country has as yet been required to publish its accounts in this way, with the result that the public is at a loss to know how it is being served. This is an omission that it is urgent to remedy.

It gives rise to two difficulties, both due to the fact that services are interdependent. The first is that certain services are provided to attract or facilitate other business, and though the charge made for them is below their cost, they amply justify themselves by adding to the revenue from other services. This difficulty is easily met. A service is uneconomical if the discontinuance of that service would reduce total costs of the undertaking more than total receipts; and it is justified if discontinuance reduces total receipts more than total costs. All that requires to be established when any particular service is challenged is how it measures up to this test.

The second difficulty is to isolate the marginal costs directly attributable to each service, distinguishing both from costs directly attributable to other services, and from the general expenses of the undertaking. The theoretical solution is straightforward, but there may sometimes be practical difficulties in drawing a line. These must not deter us. That a decision is hard to make does not absolve us from making decisions, or from ensuring that there is democratic control of decisions. The accountants will do the best that they can.

It is when we move on from the proposition that each service must cover its marginal costs to the costs that are common to all services that we get into difficulties. We have discussed this problem in a previous essay on "Fixed Costs," arguing that every undertaking must cover all its escapable costs, and that the difference between the total of escapable costs and the sum of the costs directly attributable to each service should be levied on each service in accordance with some estimate of the consumers surplus derived from each service. There is nothing new in "charging what the traffic will bear," or more appropriately, "not charging what the traffic will not bear." Public utilities practise it all over the world, and tribunals and the law have had great experience of it. The main legal problem is to distinguish between this and "undue preference," a distinction which has long been established in English railway law in more or less acceptable terms. The main political problem is to prevent special interests from using influence to escape bearing their fair share of common charges. All these problems are for a tribunal to settle. Let the public corporation fix its charges and then let anyone who considers that his burden is inequitable, or the Consumers' Council if it dislikes the general structure of the charges, make a motion before the tribunal. Difficult as these problems are, they are not new, and there is a wealth of precedent.

(The suggestion that the corporation fix its own charges should be noted. The procedure in the case of the British railways, where every charge had to be fixed or approved by the Railway Rates Tribunal proved unnecessarily cumbersome. It is better that the corporation should be free to fix its own charges, and that they should stand unless the tribunal, on motion from some aggrieved party, directs otherwise. If the public is very dissatisfied and very active, the tribunal may be used so extensively that in practice all charges come under review as soon as they are made. But it is not necessary to court so much trouble; and simpler to give the corporation freedom until challenged.)

The final problem which a tribunal may have to settle is the appropriate general level of charges. The corporation is entitled, in all circumstances, to raise enough to cover all its escapable costs, including depreciation and interest on all renewable assets. Non-renewable assets and profits and losses due to price changes are more difficult, as we have already seen in the essay on "Fixed Costs." In practice the problem presents itself in three ways. First, a corporation inherits interest payments on the stock given to the previous owners of the property. In the case of the London Transport Board an equity element was retained in some of the stock, but this retention of risk without control has obvious disadvantages, and has not been repeated. The stock of recent corporations is Government guaranteed, and the Government will expect the corporation to set its charges at a level adequate to pay the interest. provided that the concern has not been overcapitalised, this is a reasonable expectation. The public protests whenever, on account of rising costs, the general level of charges has to be raised, and the tribunal will almost always be asked to disallow the change; but if the corporation can show that the increase is needed to enable interest to be paid, the tribunal should have no right to interfere.

Secondly, a corporation may wish to build up reserves to finance expansion. Private business expands by reinvesting profits. Personal savings from income were very low in this country before the war, and but for reinvestment of profits net investment would have been small. It is therefore arguable that corporations also should be free to build up reserves for expansion. The argument is impressive. On the other hand a corporation cannot be given unlimited freedom to impose forced saving on the community simply by keeping its charges high. The best compromise is probably to set a limit; to provide that a sum not exceeding x per cent of turnover may be put to reserve in any year after all other charges have been met (including in charges a reasonable reserve against future deficits, and repayment to the Exchequer of past deficits), to require prices to be adjusted so that the surplus shall not exceed this sum, and in order to remove any incentive to estimate wrongly, to provide that any excess over this sum in any year shall be paid to the Exchequer (which would have had to meet any corresponding deficit on interest payments).

Thirdly and similarly, a corporation may wish to set up a sinking fund to redeem existing capital obligations. The London Passenger Transport Board was required to do this by law. This is a hangover from municipal trading; the townspeople, having established their gasworks by borrowing, were anxious to stop the drain to outside lenders, and in effect levied upon themselves enough saving to make the gasworks their own. In the context of national enterprises financed by internal borrowing this has less meaning. Nevertheless it is not unreasonable for the consumers of a commodity to wish to be able to own the undertaking that produces it, and thus to escape an annual interest payment. The real point is that in either case, municipal or national, consumers who feel that way are free to save and buy the corporation's stock, and it is hard on consumers who do not feel that way, and who would prefer to put their savings to other purposes, that they should be compelled to this forced saving. A corporation should not be compelled by law to establish a sinking fund; it may have permissive powers, but their exercise should be subject to agreement by the Consumers' Council.

In sum, every Act creating a public corporation needs a lengthy section controlling the economic policy of the corporation, and giving to the corporation's tribunal power to protect the public interest. Labour Ministers have been rejecting this conclusion in their desire to give to corporations as much freedom as possible. They should remember that freedom for corporations may spell tyranny for the public.

III

EFFICIENCY

The biggest problem of public corporations is efficiency. It is not yet established that they can in this sense deliver the goods, and unless they are able to disprove the assertions of those who maintain that public enterprise must always be unenterprising, bureaucratic and costly, the British public will sooner or later rid itself of them.

The first principle to be applied here is to avoid unnecessary centralisation. When an industry is being nationalised it is not always necessary to hand it over to a single public corporation to be operated under central control, and this should never be done unless there are clear advantages of centralisation. There is, for example, a clear case for having a single body operating a telephone system throughout the country, or generating electricity and maintaining a national grid; but there is no case for having a single authority in charge of coal mines, gas works, or motor transport. If the industry is to be nationalised, it will often be desirable that there be created not one public corporation but several, independent of each other, or at least only loosely connected.

It is nevertheless inevitable that public corporations will be large, and thus beset by all the administrative problems that affect large undertakings. A public corporation has open to it the usual devices on which all large concerns must rely in order to retain alertness—research, decentralisation, good personnel management, piece rates, and the like. The public is vitally interested in efficiency, as the corporation has the right to charge prices as high as are needed to cover its costs. And yet, there is little control that can be exercised. The most important control is for the Minister to pick good administrators—irrespective of party—and to remove those who do not come up to the standard. Corporation Directors should be subject to dismissal without notice. So far, Parliament has not wished to accept this principle, fearing political influences, but political influences or no, it simply does not make sense to give to key officers almost unrestricted security of tenure; the community just cannot afford it.

Subject to this control the Directors must be left freedom to economise as they think best. All the same the public should be given information which enables it to test the result. Financial accounts are essential, but they are not enough since even the most inefficient concern may be able to make a profit if it has a monopoly. The most important type of information is comparative cost statistics. Corporations should be required to publish their returns in such a way that full light is thrown on their costs. Where there are different units performing similar operations, such as different factories, or separate coal mines, or different lines of railway, the costs of each unit should be shown separately, so that the public may see the range of efficiency in the undertaking, and also be safeguarded against a natural tendency for inefficient units to be kept going and subsidised by the more efficient ones. The Consumers' Council should examine these figures every year, compare the results of the Corporations where there is more than one in the field, compare all the British figures with what similar statistics it can get for other countries, discuss doubtful questions with the Boards, and report to the Minister, who, if persuaded that the best is not being done, should in the last resort exercise his right to change the Board.

The public has also the right to insist on public corporations taking special steps to win over that loyalty of employees without which efficient service is impossible. This raises two special issues, relations with trade unions, and workers participation in management.

The nationalisation of an industry increases the individual worker's need to be protected by a strong trade union, since he is now faced by a single employer instead of several, and if he loses his job he cannot look elsewhere within the same industry. At the same time, the trade union is in practice greatly strengthened. Two powerful forces meet in a nationalised industry, a single employer and a strong trade union, and the outcome of their clash is of the greatest public interest, whether it results in a disorganising strike, or in excessive wage concessions at the expense of prices and the public. Indeed, the public interest is too large any longer to be left at the mercy of voluntary negotiations between the corporation and the union, from which it is excluded. Compulsory arbitration of disputes would seem to be fully justified, with penalties against individuals who thereafter take it upon themselves to advise or procure defiance of an arbitral award. This in turn is not desirable without laying down general principles for the guidance of arbitration tribunals, on wages, hours, and the other dissatisfactions that produce disputes. It requires not just a "wages policy," but a general code of fair employment practice. We have reached a stage where such codes can be constructed, and this step cannot be long postponed. It will not, however, be attempted in this essay, for it would take us far beyond the scope of the public corporation.

Workers participation in managerial decisions must begin not at the centre but at the periphery. Central participation has little effect; the worker at the bench is not particularly moved on learning that Sir Steward Shop or Lord Union, a prominent union secretary, has been appointed to a board of management at a lofty salary: neither is he much interested in annual elections where scores or hundreds of thousands of workers choose half a dozen men to sit on managerial committees. Such people are too remote. What interests him is his own participation, or at least that of one of the dozen or so other employees whom he knows pretty well. Corporations must decentralise to the utmost practicable limit, so as to permit the utmost practicable participation of workers in whatever decisions and recommendations can be made at the periphery. Decentralisation further permits group loyalties to be more easily created. A man may have little loyalty to an immense corporation, but will take an interest in the work of his own pit, or shop, or branch. Results for each small unit must be recorded separately and compared; "socialist competition" must be stimulated by setting each unit a weekly or monthly or annual target, publishing results, and rewarding those units which most exceed their targets. Contemporary discussion in England lays greater emphasis on piece rates and bonus systems to awaken individual desire. These too are useful, but the special opportunity of the public corporation is to awaken and make the fullest use of the social spirit, and it should not neglect it. Workers must be made to feel that they are taking part in something very special.

No statutory provision is needed on workers' participation. The real safeguard of the workers is their trade unions, which are most competent to consider and report on such matters. It is for them to discuss with the Board any points of difference, and to report to the Minister any suggestions on which there is firm disagreement, leaving him free to intervene or not, as he thinks fit. The relations between the Board, the unions and the workers are crucial. The problems to which they give rise have not yet been faced squarely in any public corporation. New techniques remain to be worked out.

IV

PARTIAL SOCIALISATION

So far we have been assuming that the corporation is given a monopoly of its industry. If it is not given a monopoly but is competing with private firms, additional rules are required to ensure that this competition shall be reasonable. All the public corporations as yet established are monopolies, but many people, including many non-socialists, would welcome the establishment of Government enterprises in some industries, without any restrictions on private business, if only to act as a check on private monopoly power. We are not concerned in this essay to discuss the merits of such matters; our business is merely with the rules that should govern corporations once the decision has been taken to create them.

If a public corporation is established in competition with private firms, care must be taken to ensure that competition shall be fair. This has two aspects; first that the corporation should not

N

receive specially favourable (or unfavourable) treatment, and secondly that its prices should be competitive.

The corporation may receive discriminatory treatment at the hands of the Government, the trade unions, or the general public. The Government may discriminate in several ways. The corporation should be subject to exactly the same taxes as private firms. It should receive no favouritism in the allocation of sites, of raw materials, of borrowing powers, or of labour. And it should receive no favouritism even in the allocation of Government contracts. It is obvious that the "yard stick" purposes of a corporation are nullified if any of these rules is broken, and at the same time private competing firms are given a just grievance. The difficulty, in practice, is to execute these rules. The civil servants who administer allocations and controls have their prejudices, whether for or against public trading; where there is nothing to choose between claimants, their prejudices may operate either for or against the corporation; or even in straining over backwards to be fair, they may act unfairly. The most that we can do is to be sure that there is adequate process of appeal against decisions in which favouritism is possible, whether for or against the corporation.

How important trade union discrimination can be is shown by the consumers' co-operative movement. Until recently the employees of the movement belonged to a separate union from other employees in the distributive trades. And the co-operatives were required—and still are—to pay much higher wages than are paid by private shopkeepers. Such competition cannot be fair. If trade unions believe in public enterprise they must agree that all employers should pay the same rates, whether private or public, and arbitration tribunals should decide in the light of this principle.

As for the general public, it also has its prejudices. The success of every firm depends on building up public goodwill, and clearly the public corporation must have the same right to build up goodwill by advertising and other methods as any private firm. Included in this must be the right to solicit patronage on the ground that it is public enterprise; just as private firms will have the right to seek the patronage of those who specially want to support private enterprise. The issue between private and public enterprise should be decided by the general public, and the clearest decision will be recorded by the relative support received by competing private and public undertakings.

What the corporation may not do is to charge prices below cost in order to drive its competitors out of business, and relying on Government subsidy (including low interest charges) to cover its losses. This is more difficult to regulate than it seems, because the correct price policy is not easily laid down.

In static economic conditions it would be simple to require the corporation to cover all its escapable costs, and its hold on the market would be determined simply by its efficiency, compared with the efficiency of private firms. There would still be the problem that in an imperfect market some big private company might set out to render the corporation bankrupt by running a price war, selling below cost for a considerable period in the hope that the public corporation would be wound up, and monopolistic prices once more be restored. There would have to be powers to cope with this—either by allowing the corporation to sell below cost and meet its rival on its own terms until the war was called off, or preferably by some impartial Government agency forbidding this kind of tactic. This kind of problem is not insoluble. What it requires is that in these mixed industries with public and private firms competing, there must be a tribunal to which complaint of charging below cost can be taken by either side, the tribunal to intervene only if the defendant's price is less not only than his own cost but also than the plaintiff's cost (i.e. a firm may sell below cost if others are more efficient than itself, but not otherwise).

The biggest difficulties spring from the fact that economic conditions are not static. There are both cyclical and secular movements in prices and costs.

A corporation cannot be ordered always to charge prices covering long run escapable costs because during the slump when demand is low its rivals will get all the business by basing their prices on short run escapable costs. On the other hand, if the corporation is just left free to adjust its prices according to the circumstances of the moment, there is bound to be endless complaint that it is undercutting and selling below cost. If industries were perfectly competitive it could just be left to follow the market; but industries are not perfectly competitive, and in practice a corporation would always be able to exercise considerable influence on prices.

Whatever the corporation does in the slump, whether it maintains prices or lowers them, is certain to cause trouble unless it acts in concert with the private firms in the industry. Neither is it desirable that, in an industry where the actions of individual firms greatly affect the market, they should pursue temporary price policies of a warlike nature during a slump, each following its individual bent—disorganised and desultory price cutting has deflationary consequences for the economic system as a whole, if it occurs just when business prospects seem uncertain. When the slump comes, and demand falls off temporarily, corporation and private firms should agree on some common policy, to be sanctioned and enforced by the tribunal. This policy may be for reduction of prices or for their stabilisation, according to circumstances; e.g. there is a prima facie case for reducing prices in heavy and constructional industries during the slump which does not apply to consumers' goods industries. A tribunal can consider all the facts, including the Government's views and anti-cyclical policy, and lay down a common price policy for the industry.

The same arguments apply to secular changes. If demand falls off permanently in an industry whose resources are immobile, a long period of price cutting may prove very damaging to the industry, and it may be desirable to have instead a reorganisation scheme for rapid adjustment of supply to demand. Here again policy requires co-operation between the corporation and the private firms. Fair competition is impossible, at times of special stress, without co-operation.

V

CONCLUSION

We may summarise by bringing together the principal points where current practice falls short of what is desirable.

1. Every corporation needs to be subject to a tribunal on services and charges, to which complaints may be referred, and whose decisions must be final, subject to legal appeal. The tribunal itself should be bound by certain general principles relating price and cost.

2. A single corporation should not be given control over an entire industry unless there are special advantages in central control. It is frequently more efficient to create several corporations rather than a single corporation.

3. Consumers' Councils have much work to do; to approach the tribunal on services and charges; to study cost statistics and

efficiency; and to report to the Minister at least once a year on matters arising. For such work they need a competent full-time staff.

4. The Minister will appoint the Boards of Directors, decide questions of subsidisation, and receive reports from the Boards, from the Consumers' Council, and from trade unions. The subject matter of these reports should be within the competence of Parliamentary debate, but not the matters of price and service which are settled by the tribunal.

5. The corporation should publish full data on costs, in forms prescribed by the Minister, as well as the usual financial returns.

6. In partial socialisation there must be a code of fair competition, and a tribunal to enforce it.

INDEX

For Product Safety Concerns and Information please contact our EU
representative GPSR@taylorandfrancis.com Taylor & Francis Verlag GmbH,
Kaufingerstraße 24, 80331 München, Germany

Printed and bound by CPI Group (UK) Ltd, Croydon, CR0 4YY
08/05/2025
01864349-0001